VEGAN
ON A BUDGET

Also by Nava Atlas

COOKBOOKS

Plant-Powered Protein

5-Ingredient Vegan

Plant Power

Wild About Greens

Vegan Holiday Kitchen

Vegan Soups and Hearty Stews for All Seasons

Vegan Express

The Vegetarian Family Cookbook

The Vegetarian 5-Ingredient Gourmet

Great American Vegetarian

Vegetarian Express

Vegetarian Celebrations

Vegetariana

VISUAL NONFICTION

The Literary Ladies' Guide to the Writing Life

Secret Recipes for the Modern Wife

Expect the Unexpected When You're Expecting! (A Parody)

VEGAN
ON A BUDGET

125 HEALTHY, WALLET-FRIENDLY, PLANT-BASED RECIPES

NAVA ATLAS

STERLING EPICURE
New York

STERLING EPICURE
New York

An Imprint of Sterling Publishing Co., Inc.
122 Fifth Avenue
New York, NY 10011

ISBN 978-1-4549-3697-8
ISBN 978-1-4549-3698-5 (e-book)

Distributed in Canada by Sterling Publishing Co., Inc.
c/o Canadian Manda Group, 664 Annette Street
Toronto, Ontario M6S 2C8, Canada
Distributed in the United Kingdom by GMC Distribution Services
Castle Place, 166 High Street, Lewes, East Sussex BN7 1XU, England
Distributed in Australia by NewSouth Books
University of New South Wales, Sydney, NSW 2052, Australia

For information about custom editions, special sales,
and premium and corporate purchases, please contact
Sterling Special Sales at 800-805-5489 or
specialsales@sterlingpublishing.com.

Manufactured in China

2 4 6 8 10 9 7 5 3 1

sterlingpublishing.com

Cover design by David Ter-Avanesyan
Interior design by Christine Heun
Photography credits on page 206

CONTENTS

INTRODUCTION

One of the best things we can do for our own health and our warming planet is to go vegan. But there's a lingering conception (admittedly, sometimes true) that plant-based fare involves esoteric and expensive ingredients. Whole ingredients and organic produce can, indeed, be pricier than mass-produced foods, but this collection of recipes will prove that you don't have to choose between healthy and inexpensive.

With a multitude of good reasons to go vegan, the plant-based movement seems to have reached a tipping point. No longer is being vegan a sign of weirdness (as merely being a vegetarian was not so long ago); instead, it has become a badge of honor. Many young people are going vegan, wisely recognizing that reducing our dependence on animal agriculture can help mitigate the rapid warming of the planet. The younger demographic also cares deeply about the ethical aspect of using animals as food. As we climb the ladder of years, interest in the plant-based diet seems more focused on how it affects our health.

Yet all these interests are fluid, and overlap. Many veterans of plant-based eating are committed to ethical veganism, opposing the exploitation of animals. Younger people alarmed by the climate crisis also recognize and appreciate the nutritional aspect of the plant-based diet. There's a lot of room in this continuum. Even if you're just exploring and not ready to take the plunge full time, consider joining the movement, even if it means easing into it with just a few vegan meals a week.

One thing that has made a huge difference in people's willingness to explore the plant-based diet is that there is no longer anything you need to give up. There's a way to make vegan versions of practically anything these days, things that couldn't be remotely imagined not long ago (hello, plant-based seafood!). You can still have burgers, pizza, egglike dishes, creamy casseroles, delectable desserts, and other crave-worthy comfort foods. And the options are expanding and improving all the time. You'll find dozens of recipes of this kind of familiar fare in this book—dishes that are easy to prepare and that your entire household will love.

Much of this introduction will assume that you're new (or at least new-ish) to plant-based eating and are looking for information on setting up your kitchen and pantry. Others might be more familiar with vegan food, but looking for ways to be more efficient and save money; if this describes you, there are plenty of tips ahead. Otherwise, if you're simply looking for fresh inspiration for everyday meals, feel free to skip ahead and begin to explore the bountiful yet frugal recipes in the chapters ahead.

PLANT-BASED MEAL PLANNING TIPS TO SAVE YOU MONEY (AND TIME)

Planning meals for the week not only saves time and money, but restores sanity. This is true whether you're single, part of a couple or family, or a member of a collection of roommates. The goal is to make last-minute shopping trips, expensive convenience foods, makeshift meals, and take-out dinners the exception rather than the rule. Here are a few basic tips to help make that happen.

Plan three meals per week that will yield leftovers. No matter what the size of your household, get in the habit of making ample meals so you can count on leftovers for three more dinners, or at least enough to supply the next day's portable lunch. Taking lunch to school or work from home can save you hundreds, if not thousands, of dollars a year.

Dinner leftovers can be tweaked so that they're slightly different the next day. For example, today's salad can be tomorrow's wrap; tonight's soup-and-wrap dinner can become tomorrow's soup-and-vegan quesadilla dinner. Grain dishes can be stuffed into vegetables or made into wraps with leafy lettuces. And the seventh day can be the wild card—make something special (or not so special), have a breakfast-y dinner, or invite friends over for a potluck!

Get in the meal-planning habit by being consistent. If you find yourself doing catch-as-catch-can more than you'd like, try doing your meal planning and food shopping on the same day each week. This can be once or twice a week, depending on your need and schedule, and the size of your household. Browse your favorite cookbooks or blogs, and ask other members of your household to participate and offer ideas on what kinds of meals they look forward to.

Planning meals before you go food shopping helps ensure that you don't waste time, money, and energy running back and forth to the store all week. One meal-planning session per week will simplify your life immeasurably, especially if you have a tight schedule, young children, or both.

At first, it might be challenging to set aside time for a regular meal-planning session that includes making a shopping list. If you do your grocery shopping on the weekend, that might mean making your meal plans on Friday night or Saturday morning. You'll be amazed at how much time is saved by a 20-minute meal-planning and shopping list–making session. Stock your pantry and freezer with basic ingredients. Making sure that your pantry and freezer are stocked with healthy staples will go a long way toward making meal decisions less stressful. It's much easier to tackle meal prep when your kitchen is stocked with useful staples. Even when you haven't planned ahead—and we all have those kind of days—

there will be something great to fall back on at home. Think of easy pizzas, wraps, or vegan burgers accompanied by coleslaw and/or steamed veggies that take minutes to prepare. To get started, explore Stocking Your Pantry with the Basics (page xvi).

Prepare a few basics for the week ahead. On whatever day or evening you're most likely to find yourself at home, prepare a few basics for the days ahead. Often, Sunday afternoons or evenings are ideal as you're looking forward to the coming week, but be prepared to adapt to whatever fits your schedule.

Prepping even a few simple food items ahead of time can make the weeknight dinner routine so much easier. Knowing that you have even one item that's already prepared when you enter the kitchen at dinnertime or later is a great feeling, and the rest of the meal will come together more easily. Here are some things you can do:

■ Bake or microwave potatoes, sweet potatoes, or winter squashes.

■ Cook some quinoa, brown rice, and/or other grains.

■ Clean, stem, and chop kale, collards, or other sturdy greens and store them in an airtight container.

■ Soak and cook beans (if you prefer cooking them from scratch).

■ Make hummus or another kind of dip or spread to use in sandwiches and wraps.

■ Prep for cooking a few sturdy vegetables that keep well: Cut broccoli and/or cauliflower into small florets; stem and halve Brussels sprouts; pre-bake winter squashes.

■ Cut up a variety of healthy, easy-to-grab fresh veggies and fruits that keep well, like peppers, carrots, grapes, and pears, and that can be used as snacks or tossed into salads.

■ Make homemade salad dressings.

At least once a week, prepare a big one-pot or one-pan meal. Hearty soups or stews, bean and pasta dishes, and casseroles are the kinds of meals that can stretch to two dinners, sometimes more. You'll find plenty of these dishes in the chapters ahead. Double recipes if you're part of a larger household or want to freeze part of what you make for future meals. Use weekly repertoires. If you still find meal-making to be a bit daunting, try getting a little more regimented. You can still make slight variations on your weekly meal lineup to shake things up a bit and keep it all less predictable, so that meals don't get boring. It's like that old commercial, where Wednesday was always spaghetti day. These kinds of routines can also make life feel more orderly and organized. For example, your week could look something like this:

■ Sunday could be the day to make that big soup or stew that will stretch over at least a couple of nights, as well as provide extra portions for lunches and possible freezing.

■ On Monday, you'll enjoy the fruits of Sunday's

cooking. For example, if you have leftover soup, it can be served with sandwiches and/or salad, depending on everyone's appetites.

▪ Tuesday that soup is still looking good, so finish it up, and serve it with simple wraps or vegan quesadillas.

▪ Wednesday can indeed be spaghetti day, but let's stretch that definition to include any kind of pasta, even Asian noodles. Simply prepared veggies and/or salads can be served on the side.

▪ Thursday's meal can be your household's favorite kind of restaurant food, but in easy, homemade versions. Tex-Mex-style tortilla dishes are so easy to make at home; so are stir-fries and curries. Keep a few favorite recipes on hand that you can rotate through the month.

▪ Friday is for kicking back. Maybe it's an at-home movie or binge-watching your favorite series. The perfect accompaniment is an almost-instant pizza with fresh veggies. Or, vegan burgers and fries (or oven-roasted potatoes or sweet potatoes) comprise another kind of meal that's easy to make in healthy plant-based form.

▪ As mentioned earlier, Saturday is your wild card day. You could be joining friends for dinner at their place or yours, or cleaning up this week's leftovers.

This is just one example of a weekly meal repertoire. Make your meal plans your own, centering them on the kinds of meals and foods you and the other members of your household enjoy most.

BE A SMART FOOD SHOPPER

The ideal plant-based diet centers around whole foods, as close to their original state as possible. Grains, beans, vegetables, fruits, nuts, and seeds are the foundations. Minimally processed plant proteins (like tofu, tempeh, and seitan) are staples as well. When the goal is to eat better, the first step in that direction is to shop wisely, especially if you're on a budget.

Before going food shopping, no matter where you decide to shop, see what's already in your pantry and fridge. You'll save money by avoiding duplication of foods in your kitchen. I know this because I don't always follow my own advice. Not long ago, I bought a red cabbage, forgetting that there was almost a whole one still in the fridge. Cabbage keeps well, but seriously, there's just so much red cabbage that can be used in one go. I'm also the expert at buying jars of salsa when I see a two-for-a-certain-price sale, forgetting that I already have four jars in the pantry. Salsa keeps and always gets used up, but still, it's not a good practice to overbuy when you're trying to follow a food budget. Taking a quick survey of what you already have is always a good strategy before your shopping trips.

THE SUPERMARKET

First, let's upend a couple of tired food-shopping clichés:

Stick to the periphery (actually, don't). We've all heard this one: Concentrate on the periphery of the store. And while this might be somewhat true, it also means that you'd be missing out on some important vegan staples.

The periphery of supermarkets is where you'll find the produce section, which, in recent years, has expanded quite a bit in many stores to include tofu, tempeh, and other plant proteins. It's where you'll also be likely to find the growing array of nondairy milks, vegan butter, and the like.

But if you only shop on the periphery, you'll miss out on many vegan foundation foods in the inner aisles, notably pastas, grains, and beans. Then, there's the frozen foods aisle, which holds an array of simple, flash-frozen vegetables that can help stretch your food budget. And the international foods aisle is an especially good source for sauces and condiments that take homemade meals from so-so to amazing.

Finally, many larger supermarkets now have natural foods aisles and bulk food sections with whole grains, legumes, nuts, seeds, dried fruits, and other foods that can spare you a trip to the natural foods store. So, please, look beyond the periphery (has anyone really ever followed that advice anyway?).

Stick to your list (actually, be flexible). This might seem to contradict the meal-planning tips given earlier, but it's all about flexibility. My local supermarket seems to have a fair amount of Buy One, Get One Free sales, especially in the produce department, so I rarely pass up specials on otherwise expensive items, like baby greens or blueberries. In fact, if you find these kinds of sales for any foods you like, take them home and plan dishes around those ingredients. You can also freeze sale items for later use. Conversely, what if something on your list seems unusually pricey on a certain shopping trip? Skip it and shift gears.

There's a related cliché that warns against grocery shopping while hungry. I can see why that might be good advice. It's no fun to shop when the stomach is rumbling, and lack of patience can result in hasty decisions and, hence, a higher grocery bill.

And now, here are a few more tried-and-true supermarket shopping tips:

Use coupons wisely. If you clip coupons, make sure they're for items you really need. Most coupons are for packaged foods. Coupons for fresh produce and natural foods get the least amount of marketing dollars (when was the last time you saw coupons for apples?), though there *are* ways to obtain them. More on that ahead.

Some supermarkets offer price-matching, letting shoppers use competitor's coupons for many items. Other supermarkets allow shoppers to combine store and manufacturers' coupons for the same item. Check your supermarket's website for coupon regulations and to see if there are coupons of interest to print before going shopping. As always, think through whether you really need the items being offered.

Some stores even have apps that help shoppers find coupons and daily deals. Sometimes a barcode is provided that can be scanned at checkout.

If you enjoy certain brands, go directly to the company's website for coupons. Some will require you to join their email list to receive coupons and notifications of specials. There are also sites offering printable coupons; to find certain brands, do a search on "[brand name] coupons" and the current month and year.

Look down at the bottom shelves. Companies pay more for eye-level shelf positions. The bottom shelf might be a source of cheaper goods and sale items.

Explore cut-rate supermarket chains. Shopping at different stores for various food categories can yield some savings if you have the time and patience. Cut-rate markets like Aldi and WinCo may not be the best for produce, but for other food categories, they're a good source for bargains. For example, Aldi's plant-based proteins (like vegan meatballs), made under the company's proprietary label, cost far less than other national brands. Other discount grocery chains include Fareway and Big Lots. See what's in your area, and overlook the bare-bones atmosphere for some sweet savings.

Buy fresh produce in season. This seems like it would be obvious, but with markets offering cantaloupe in January and butternut squash in July, seasonality has been blurred. Most fresh produce still has a true season—asparagus in late spring, blueberries in midsummer, winter squashes in...winter, of course. This kind of eating is not only intuitive, but produce is better—and less expensive—in its true season.

THE NATURAL FOODS STORE

Though well-stocked supermarkets now carry lots of items that were once the exclusive domain of natural foods stores, there are still many foods that are easier to find in natural foods stores. Yes, they can be more expensive than supermarkets, but not necessarily, if you shop carefully. Here are some things to keep in mind:

■ Many natural foods companies offer coupons online. If you like certain brands of good-quality packaged items, like vegan cheeses, tofu, canned beans, and such, check the company's website.

■ Compare prices between stores. Prices can vary quite a bit from one natural foods store to the next. The one in my town has prices that are an average of 20 percent lower than a store just 10 miles away.

■ Bulk bin buying can be cost-effective. Why buy packaged brown rice or quinoa, for example, when you can get them for half the price in bulk? Grains, beans, flours, lentils, nuts, seeds, dried fruits, and granola all can be bought in bulk, but there is no need to go crazy and buy 10 pounds of a certain item. Buy what you'll use within a month or two. Even dry foods, like grains or lentils, can go rancid. Buy bulk items in an active store, where regular turnover ensures that what you're buying is fresh.

■ Get a few quart mason jars to store your bulk purchases. You'll remember that you have them and will be more likely to use them when they're in your line of vision.

■ Pay attention to natural foods stores' circulars. While they may not offer coupons, these store circulars announce weekly discounts. These savings can be significant. Of course, the key to these savings is to buy only items that you actually need, just as with coupons.

■ Take advantage of special ordering. If your local natural foods store has limited shelf space, most will special-order items for you.

FINDING NATURAL FOODS COUPONS ONLINE

Some food bloggers partner with natural foods companies to offer weekly discounts and coupons as well as advice for eating healthy on a budget. Others aggregate weekly deals that you can learn about by subscribing to their newsletters or getting into the habit of doing a weekly check-in. I hesitate to list particular websites here, because, as we know, online resources have a tendency to come and go. Do a search for "natural foods coupons" and you'll find a plethora of up-to-date resources. It takes a bit of patience, but a little time invested can yield substantial savings.

You can also subscribe to the newsletters of your favorite brands. Earthbound Farm®, an organic vegetable distributor, for example, has a newsletter that's a great resource for coupons as well as simple recipes and tips.

BEST PROTEIN BARGAINS

Chances are, if you've gone vegan and share that news with a nonvegan, you'll be asked, "How do you get your protein?" It's a question that just won't go away, and it's curious that there's still so much bewilderment over how vegans get protein. The myth that it's hard to get adequate protein on a vegan diet is tenacious. There's plenty of evidence that a varied whole foods diet with sufficient calories has little chance of falling short in the protein department.

Many foods have at least some protein. Whole grains, legumes, soy foods, plant-based meat alternatives, nuts, and seeds all offer high-quality protein. Many common vegetables have small amounts of protein, too, so if you eat plenty of them, they contribute to your daily total, as well. The body can manufacture all but 9 of the 22 amino acids that make up proteins. These 9 amino acids are referred to as "essential" amino acids and must be derived from food. That is why getting sufficient, good-quality protein is crucial. The operative word here is *sufficient*—this isn't a case where more is necessarily better. The Western diet usually provides twice as much protein as needed. Here's a rundown of common plant proteins and what they supply.

Beans and Legumes

Chickpeas, black beans, pinto beans, brown lentils, and other common legume varieties contain 6 to 8 grams of protein per half-cup cooked serving. Split peas have 8 to 10 grams per half-cup serving, and red lentils have an impressive 13 grams. Beans and legumes are so blessedly low in calories and fat, that if you need more protein and have the capacity, a 1-cup serving isn't unreasonable.

Tofu, Tempeh, and Seitan

Here are the protein amounts per servings listed:

Tofu, firm: 4 ounces = 10 grams

Tofu, extra-firm: 4 ounces = 8 grams

Tofu, baked: 2 ounces = 11 grams

Tempeh: 4 ounces = 20 to 21 grams

Seitan: 4 ounces = 28 grams

Nuts

Nuts are, admittedly, a bigger-ticket item, especially if they're organic, but they're filled with a plethora of nutrients, notably B vitamins. While we can't classify them as an inexpensive protein source, they're worth the indulgence from time to time. In this book, I primarily call for peanuts and walnuts, as those are generally the least costly. As always, look for bulk bin savings, or explore online sources.

Here are the protein amounts in ¼ cup of a few common nuts:

Almonds = 8 grams

Cashews = 5 grams

Peanuts = 7 grams

Pistachios = 6 grams

Walnuts = 4 grams

Let's not forget nut butter. Peanut butter contains a generous 8 grams of protein per 2-tablespoon serving. Cashew butter and almond butter have similar amounts, but since they can be quite expensive, the recipes in this book only call for peanut butter.

Seeds

A reasonable serving of chia, flax, hemp, pumpkin, and sunflower seeds is 2 tablespoons, and that amount gives you about 4 to 6 grams of protein.

Grains

Like legumes, whole grains are low in fat and high in fiber, and offer a multitude of B vitamins. While there are many more grain varieties than those listed below, these are the ones used most frequently in this book.

Here are the protein amounts in 1 cup of cooked grain:

Barley = 7 grams

Rice, Brown = 6 grams

Rice, White = 4.2 grams

Oatmeal (old-fashioned) cooked = 6 grams

Quinoa = 8 grams

Nutritional Yeast (Red Star®)

This bigger-ticket item is a staple for many vegans because it is a great source of vitamin B_{12} (a rare nutrient in plant foods); a 1½ tablespoon amount contains 130 percent of average daily needs, and it also supplies 8 grams of protein. Because it is costly, however, I often make it an optional ingredient in this book.

Pasta

Even ordinary pasta offers 7 grams of protein per cooked cup. Combined with beans, vegetables, nuts, tofu, and other foods, pasta does become a great protein bargain.

ORGANIC VERSUS CONVENTIONAL PRODUCE

Given the choice, I would almost always opt for organic produce. It's hard to argue with the virtues of limiting our exposure to pesticides. And let's not forget about the agricultural workers whose health is at constant risk from handling toxin-laden produce on a daily basis. A majority of shoppers buy organic foods at their primary supermarket, proving that this category of foods has moved into the mainstream. Because of demand and economies of scale, the cost differential between organic and conventional produce is narrower than it once was.

Still, there's no question that organic produce is more expensive than conventional, so it can be daunting to purchase it all the time. One way to solve this dilemma is to be aware of which crops are highest in pesticides, and which use relatively few or even no pesticides as they're produced. The way to do this is by consulting the Environmental Working Group's annual list of produce that's the most contaminated, known as The Dirty Dozen™, and its companion list of produce that's safe to consume even if they're not organic. The latter group is known as The Clean Fifteen™.

The list changes from year to year, so it's good to consult the organization's website (http://ewg.org). A few varieties of produce that seem to always make the "bad list" are strawberries, apples, and spinach. Some that are most often on the clean list include asparagus, avocado, sweet corn, cabbage, and sweet potatoes. Buying produce that's not certifiably organic but also not pesticide-laden can be a good money-saving option.

STOCKING YOUR PANTRY WITH THE BASICS

Beans and Legumes, Canned and Dried

Keeping a variety of canned beans in the pantry is one of the cornerstones of easy-to-prepare meals. They do contain a lot of sodium, but draining and rinsing them helps to mitigate that.

If canned beans are a frugal form of protein, cooking them from scratch probably makes them the most frugal protein of all. If you have a pressure cooker, a slow cooker, or an Instant Pot®, the process is even more attractive. But if you don't, all you really need is a roomy cooking pot and a little time and patience. You'll find cooking tips just ahead (page xvii). Here's a list of common legumes to choose from and the varieties mainly used in this book:

- Black beans
- Chickpeas (garbanzos)
- Great Northern beans or cannellini
- Kidney beans
- Lentils
- Navy beans
- Pink beans

Pinto beans

Red beans

Lentils merit a little more discussion. Though they don't take as long to cook from scratch as other beans, when you want dinner on demand, even the relatively quick cooking time of lentils (30 minutes or so) can give you pause. As with all beans, you can always turn to canned lentils for a little extra cost. Canned brown lentils taste good and hold their shape nicely. When you have more time and inclination to cook them from scratch, please do so! Cooking tips are on page xvii.

Tiny red lentils cook up quickly (15 to 20 minutes) to a delectably mushy texture that makes a great base for soups and stews.

How to Cook Beans

Pressure cookers, slow cookers, and Instant Pot are excellent options for cooking raw beans, and for those, you simply follow the manufacturer's directions.

For cooking beans the old-fashioned way, all you need is a large pot with a lid. The rule of thumb is that raw beans swell to about two and a half times their volume once cooked. If you need 4 cups of cooked beans, for example, start with 1⅔ cups raw (though it always pays to cook more beans than you need for just one recipe since they freeze well for later use). Here are the basic steps:

1. Rinse the beans in a colander and look through them carefully to remove grit and small stones.

2. Combine the beans with about three times their volume of water (this doesn't have to be exact) in a large pot. Cover and soak overnight. Refrigerate the beans in the pot if your kitchen tends to be warm, or if it's summer. For a quicker soaking method, bring the mixture to a boil, then cover and let stand off the heat for an hour or two.

3. Drain the beans (though some vitamins may be lost, draining off the soaking water also eliminates some of the complex sugars that make beans hard to digest for some). Fill the pot with fresh water to measure about double the volume of the beans. Tip: Peel and quarter a small onion and add it to the water. This will add flavor to the beans as they cook.

4. Bring the water to a boil, then lower the heat to a gentle simmer. Cover and cook the beans slowly and steadily. Keep the cover slightly ajar to prevent foaming. Most beans take about 1½ hours to cook slowly and thoroughly. To test if beans are done, press one between your thumb and forefinger; it should yield easily. A bit overdone is better than underdone, which will hinder their digestibility and mouthfeel.

5. Add salt only when the beans are done. Salt tends to harden the skins and prolong cooking time.

How to Cook Lentils

Unlike many other legumes, lentils don't need to be presoaked.

1. Rinse them and check for small stones.

2. Combine the lentils with about 2½ times their volume of water in a large saucepan. Bring to a slow boil, then reduce the heat to low and cover, keeping the lid ajar, to let the lentils simmer. Add more water if needed. Lentils don't need to absorb all the water they're cooked in, so you can always drain excess liquid off.

Brown or green lentils take about 30 minutes to cook. It's best to stop the cooking process when they're just tender, but still hold their shape. Beluga and de puy lentils might take slightly less time to cook. Red lentils take 15 minutes or less, and cook to a mushy consistency, so they're best used as a base for soups and stews.

No matter what kind of lentils you're cooking, check them from time to time and add more water if need be, but don't stir too much. Drain any excess water.

Grains

Whole grains add variety to meals and are great low-fat sources of fiber and protein, B vitamins, vitamin E, and an array of minerals. Since this book is all about economy, we're going to stick with a few basics when it comes to grains—mainly rice, quinoa, barley, and oats.

Whole grains are most economical bought in bulk, and I suggest buying modest quantities, perhaps a pound or two at a time. If you're going to store whole grains at room temperature, don't buy more than what you'll use up in two to three cooler months, or just one warmer month. And if you see that your grains aren't moving even that quickly, freeze them (raw) in 1 to 1½ cup portions. If your kitchen is warm during hot summer months, refrigerate your grains.

I like to store grains in clear mason jars on open kitchen shelves. Not only is this an inexpensive and nice-looking form of kitchen decor, having them out in the open is a reminder to use them!

Nondairy (aka Plant-Based) Milks

Not so long ago, there was one choice in ready-made nondairy milk (now more often being referred to as plant-based milk), and that was soy milk. And then there were two, when rice milk came on the scene. Nut milks have been made from time immemorial, and now they're also a staple in this category, especially, it seems, almond milk.

Now, there are lots of options, including almond, hemp, cashew, and coconut (the last being of the beverage iteration, not the canned variety). The newest kid on the block is oat milk, which is being touted as the most sustainable of plant-based milks, more environmentally friendly than any of the nut milks. And it's really good, too, with a natural sweetness that's easy to love.

While plant-based milks aren't big-ticket items, neither are they bargains. The best tip is to buy them in aseptic quart containers (which make them storable at room temperature until opened) rather than in half gallons so there's less chance of spoilage if not used up within a reasonable amount of time.

Nuts and Seeds

Nuts and seeds are a great source of concentrated protein in the plant-based diet, and are abundant in valuable B vitamins, vitamin E, and a wide range of minerals, including calcium, zinc, and iron. Nuts and seeds are 50–70 percent fat, but they're primarily healthy polyunsaturated and monounsaturated fats. A quarter cup (or smaller serving, in the case of seeds) is a good rule of thumb.

Admittedly, nuts and seeds are in the pricier range of plant proteins. Look for bulk bin specials, and if you find good deals, buy extra—they freeze well. The high fat content of nuts and seeds makes them prone to rancidity, so purchase only what you'll use within a month or so; if your kitchen stays warm during the summer, it's best to refrigerate nuts and seeds. Compare prices in your area with those being offered online by companies that specialize in nuts, like Jaffe Bros.

The most economical nuts are walnuts and peanuts (though be sure to buy organic peanuts if you use them regularly; growers of conventional peanuts use a lot of pesticides),

so I focus on those in this book. Almost everyone loves cashews, but, alas, they, along with pecans, are often among the priciest of nuts. If you want to enjoy cashews occasionally, look for pieces, which are less expensive than whole nuts.

Seeds are a bit more of a bargain in this category, especially pumpkin, sunflower, and sesame. Hemp and flaxseeds are nutrient powerhouses, but they are on the expensive side. I don't call for the latter two in this book, but that doesn't mean you can't enjoy them occasionally if you can stretch your food budget.

Nut Butter

Nut butter deserves a place in the plant-based pantry. Natural, organic peanut butters with no added fat, salt, or sugar are the ideal, budget-wise choice. Most other nut and seed butters are quite pricey. So for the purposes of this book, I've stuck with the all-American favorite, peanut butter. I'd still highly recommend choosing organic peanut butter for the same reason that you'd choose organic peanuts—to avoid pesticides.

Used in moderation, peanut butter is a good source of healthy fats and an array of minerals, B vitamins, and vitamin E.

Olive Oil and Other Vegetable Oils

I prefer using extra-virgin olive oil because of the extra-special flavor, but it's not always cheap,

not always on sale, and, judging from news reports, not always actually extra virgin. To get the best olive oil within your budget, be on the lookout for store coupons, but, more practically, see what brands are carried in your local stores, and do an online search for "[brand] coupon" and the current month and year.

The only other oil used in this book is neutral vegetable oil, particularly useful for high-heat stir-fries and in baked goods. My favorite is safflower oil, but there's also sunflower oil and others. These are the kinds of oils that are rich in unsaturated fatty acids, the healthier kinds of fats. Use the same strategy to find coupons online. No matter what kind you use, a little oil goes a long way. For the no-oil crowd, feel free to omit oil (which is used sparingly in the recipes to begin with) and use your favorite technique for replacing it.

Pastas and Noodles

If you're a pasta fan, keep a good supply of different sizes and shapes of pasta in your pantry. Some useful shapes are spaghetti and other long pastas (angel hair, linguine), twists (gemelli, rotini), penne, and shells. Whole grain varieties have a bit more going for them nutritionally, but even ordinary pasta, which is enriched, is a decent source of B vitamins and even protein, as discussed earlier. Gluten-free pastas have improved over the years in terms of flavor and texture, so explore them if need be.

It's hard to beat pasta for economy. A

16-ounce box is still well under $2.00 where I live. At that price, adding all kinds of vegetables and other embellishments for big, hearty pasta meals becomes quite affordable.

Noodles, like rice vermicelli and bean-thread noodles, have become easier to find in the Asian foods section of well-stocked supermarkets, and are pretty standard in natural foods stores. They're a little more expensive than ordinary pastas, but not so much as to be prohibitive for occasional use. Udon and soba start to climb a bit more in price, so here we'll stick primarily with ordinary pasta, with the occasional option of Asian noodles.

Silken Tofu

Silken tofu is a variety that can be stored in the pantry, since it comes in 12.3-ounce, aseptic packages that are shelf stable. Pureed to a smooth, silky texture, it's useful as a base to thicken soups and to make dressings, dips, and sauces. It appears occasionally in this book, and you can even use it to make a delectable Chocolate Mousse (page 176).

Soy Sauce or Tamari

Look for natural brands for the best flavor. If sodium is a concern, choose a reduced-sodium variety (which still contains plenty of sodium, mind you); gluten-free varieties are also available. The Japanese version of natural soy sauce (shoyu), made of soybeans, roasted wheat, and sea salt, is sold in natural foods stores; it's naturally fermented and has a full-bodied flavor. Tamari, also naturally fermented, is a bit stronger in flavor and thicker; it also comes in a gluten-free variety.

All varieties of soy sauce will keep nearly indefinitely, stored at room temperature. Note that mass-produced soy sauces are made with a sped-up fermentation process that doesn't allow for as fine a flavor to develop. But if you're not an aficionado, this might not be an issue for you and your taste buds.

Tomato Products

While it's always nice to use fresh tomatoes, it's not always July or August, and most of us don't have time to make our own tomato sauces from scratch. For soups, stews, and sauces, it's useful to keep a few canned tomato products on hand, including:

■ Diced, in 14-ounce cans (fire-roasted or Italian-style offer extra flavor)

■ Crushed or pureed, in 14-ounce and 28-ounce cans

■ Tomato sauce

Vinegars

Choose one or two of these vinegars to have on hand:

■ Organic apple cider vinegar—An all-purpose vinegar, choose a brand that's naturally fermented.

- Red wine or white wine vinegar—Standards for salads and making vinaigrette dressing.

- Balsamic—Also good for vinaigrettes and salads. A modest amount drizzled into roasted veggies boosts their natural sweetness.

STOCKING YOUR FREEZER

For last-minute meals and other practical purposes, these staples will always come in handy:

- Whole grain burger buns or English muffins. Useful for serving with any of the vegan burgers on pages 112 to 114.

- Whole grain pita breads and wraps. You can keep these in the fridge for some time, of course, but if you pop a package of each into the freezer, you'll have the goods to make last-minute sandwiches to pair with soup or salad for dinner. Pita can also be cut up to use for scooping up hummus.

- Good-quality pizza crusts. If your freezer can accommodate them, pizza crusts are a fantastic item to have on hand for last-minute meals that everyone loves.

- Frozen vegetables. Having green peas and corn in your freezer almost goes without saying. And since the window for good, fresh green beans is so limited, cut or whole green beans can be useful, too. Frozen items, like cauliflower (which is kind of a pain to prep after a long day at work) and shelled edamame (fresh green soybeans), might make sense

to buy occasionally for quick cooking options. Vegetables and fruits are picked at the peak of ripeness and flash-frozen, so they retain a lot of nutrients. They're a good way to stretch your produce dollars, even if you buy frozen organic.

SEASONING BLENDS FOR SAVING TIME AND MONEY

Dried herbs and spices can be downright expensive. And though they last a long time in a dry cabinet, many cooks, myself included, have a collection of bottles that do nothing but collect dust. When was the last time I used that rubbed sage that I bought in 1994?

I've become a huge fan of seasoning blends that combine lots of herbs and/or spices in one bottle. They save money by not requiring you to buy lots of different herbs and spices, and they save you time, too. Using a teaspoon or two of a seasoning blend instead of a pinch of 12 different spices can make the difference between a busy (or cash-strapped) cook wanting to tackle a recipe or looking at a long list and turning the page. Here are my favorites, and the ones used most in this book:

Barbecue seasoning: I love how this kind of seasoning packs a ton of flavor into all kinds of dishes. You'll find this kind of spice blend in well-stocked supermarkets. One of the biggest brands is McCormick Grill Mates®. While you can surmise its original purpose, it's also a boon for plant-based protein dishes, sauces, and more. Flavors include smokehouse maple, mesquite, chipotle, brown sugar bourbon—and there are lots of others. Discover your favorites, and keep a couple on hand. There are other, smaller brands of this type of seasoning that can be found in specialty stores or online.

Curry powder: There's a tendency to think of curry powder as one thing, but it's actually a blend of seasonings. Depending on brand, these can include curry, turmeric, coriander, ginger, cinnamon, cardamom, dry mustard, and others.

Italian seasoning: The one I have in my kitchen is a blend of marjoram, thyme, rosemary, savory, sage, oregano, and basil.

Salt-free seasoning: In the supermarket, one of the major brands is Mrs. Dash®, and in the natural foods store, you'll find Frontier®, Spike®, and others. They're all good, and they all use a thousand (well, maybe 15 or 20) herbs and spices, too many to list, adding up to a lively flavor and aroma. I find these salt-free seasoning blends especially useful for soups, stews, and grain pilafs.

CONVENIENT SAUCES AND CONDIMENTS

The availability of high-quality sauces and condiments can be the difference between making a simple dinner and capitulating to takeout or make-do. Not that the homemade versions are at all difficult to make, but at 7:00 p.m., you may not prefer to tackle a long list of additional ingredients in a recipe.

It may seem counterintuitive, but bottled sauces and condiments can sometimes be less expensive to buy than to make from scratch. For example, unless you're the kind of cook who keeps sesame oil, sesame seeds, mild vinegar, ginger, etc. as kitchen staples, you'd probably be better off buying a bottle of teriyaki marinade instead of all these individual ingredients to make your own. I enjoy making luscious peanut sauces on occasion, but, clearly, the savings are in the bottled store brand—even the organic version, which I prefer. Here's a listing of the kind of sauces and condiments used most often in this book:

Barbecue sauce: Departing from their original intent, sweet-and-savory barbecue sauces have so many uses in the plant-based kitchen. They're wonderful for flavoring tofu, tempeh, and seitan. All this being said, I still prefer to make my own barbecue sauce, Super-Quick No-Cook Barbecue Sauce (page 202). If you find a brand you like at a reasonable price, go for it.

Indian simmer sauce: To create the kind of complex flavors characteristic of authentic Indian dishes, a couple of spoonfuls of curry powder really doesn't cut it. Indian simmer sauces, one of the newer kinds of ready-made sauces on the market, have been a game-changer. You'll find them in the international foods aisles in supermarkets and natural foods stores.

They come in a range of vegan options, including Goan coconut, Kashmir curry, Jalfrezi, and Madras curry. Their flavors range from mild to spicy. Some include dairy, so be sure to read the labels. The main ingredients in the vegan sauces are coconut milk, tomato, ginger, garlic, and, of course, lots of spices. These sauces will infuse your homemade curries with the delicious flavors you've come to love at fine Indian restaurants.

Marinara sauce: For quick pizzas and easy pasta dishes, keep a couple of 28-ounce jars on hand. There are many flavors available; choose a variety that pleases your palate with ingredients like garlic, wine, mushrooms, peppers, vegetables, and herbs. Or, make your choice according to what's on sale! Just make sure to choose brands without nonvegan ingredients, sugar, or high-fructose corn syrup.

Salsa: Salsa comes in a nice range of varieties, and has so many uses other than being a great dip. On a budget, it can be used as a flavor booster in soups, stews, grain dishes, vegan burgers, and more. For a change of pace, try pineapple, mango, or smoky chipotle salsa. There's also salsa verde, made of piquant tomatillos.

Thai peanut satay sauce: Available in the Asian foods aisle of well-stocked supermarkets and natural foods stores, this sauce adds a blast of flavor to Asian-style noodle, vegetable, and tofu dishes. It contains several ingredients that most of us don't have on hand, including tamarind paste, kaffir lime, and lemongrass.

Other condiments and flavorings used frequently in this book are sriracha, vegan mayo, and lemon and lime juice (which you can use bottled or freshly squeezed). As you leaf through (and hopefully make) the recipes in this book, you'll notice that many of the ingredients are used over and over again. For a budget-wise kitchen that really works well, using certain ingredients in different ways but with regularity ensures that nothing gets wasted. It's more efficient to utilize a smaller group of favorite ingredients than to buy dozens of ingredients that rarely see the light of day.

DON'T WASTE GOOD FOOD!

Millions of tons of wasted food ends up in landfills in the United States each year. Not only is this a sad fact, given that so many people still go hungry, it's polluting and contributes to greenhouse gases that exacerbate climate change. And, of course, wasted food is a terrible use of your grocery budget. Here are a few ways you can reduce food waste:

Freeze your lingering leftovers. Nearly any cooked food can be put in an airtight container and popped into the freezer. If you see that a leftover hasn't been used for more than two days, it might be time to transfer it. You'll be glad to defrost it at a later date when you're in need of a quick meal.

Are your bananas getting overripe? Mash them to make yummy baked goods (see

Crunchy Granola Banana Muffins, page 183), or slice and freeze them to make Frozen Banana Ice Cream (page 187).

Don't let your fresh herbs spoil food. Store them properly by placing a fresh bunch, stems down, in a narrow glass filled with water (just as you would cut flowers). Drape a plastic bag over the bunch and store in the door of the refrigerator, where it will keep much longer. Once your herbs start getting tired, stem and chop them, then store them in the freezer in tiny individual containers to use in soups and stews. Or, if you want to use a big bunch at once, make pesto.

Put mushy tomatoes to work. Puree or finely chop tomatoes that are getting soft and combine them with marinara sauce to make a pasta or pizza sauce to use right away.

Turn grapes into neat ice cubes. Grapes that are on their way to oblivion make lovely ice cubes (or should we call them ice orbs?) for all kinds of beverages.

Deal with your leafy greens right away. We all have good intentions when it comes to leafy greens, be it spinach, kale, collards, and the like, but they're often pushed to the back of the fridge until they can't be salvaged. It's best to at least wash, dry, and chop them before just stashing them in the fridge to ensure that they'll be used quickly. If they'll be going into a cooked dish, you can also wilt them down, in which case they'll take up a lot less room in the refrigerator and will be completely ready to use when you need them.

Turn tired vegetables into stir-fries or soup stocks. Vegetables that have seen their better days aren't ideal in terms of flavor and texture, but as long as they're not spoiled, it's better to use them than lose them. Once every week or two, go through your crisper and make a big stir-fry or a homemade vegetable stock for your next pot of soup.

Now that you've got your pantry set up and a few tips in hand, I hope you'll find that making inexpensive, delicious plant-based dishes is easier and more fun than you ever imagined. Let's get cooking!

1

EVERYONE LOVES SOUPS & STEWS

Who doesn't love a bowl of warming, comforting soup or a thick stew? A big pot full of either can be the basis of a satisfying, inexpensive meal. This chapter offers a range of hearty bowlfuls, from budget-friendly favorites, like Italian Pasta & Bean Soup (page 5), to a hearty curried stew. Filled with nourishing ingredients, like grains, beans, noodles, and plenty of vegetables, soups and stews exemplify economy and comfort in perfect harmony.

Sweet Potato
& Black Bean Soup

6 servings

Here's a soup that offers up big flavor with relatively few ingredients and not a lot of cooking time. Serve tortilla chips and guacamole with this soup for a simple meal. Sliced oranges in season add a refreshing finish.

3 medium or 2 large sweet potatoes, peeled and diced (see Note)

2 (15-ounce) cans black beans, drained and rinsed, or 3 cups cooked beans

1 (28-ounce) can diced tomatoes, preferably fire-roasted

2 vegetable bouillon cubes

2 scallions, thinly sliced

½ cup salsa, your favorite variety

2 teaspoons chili powder or barbecue seasoning (for more information, see page xxii) or more, to taste

Salt and freshly ground pepper, to taste

2 to 3 ounces (2 to 3 big handfuls) baby spinach or other baby greens

½ cup cilantro leaves

1. Combine the sweet potatoes with just enough water to cover in a soup pot. Bring to a slow boil, then lower the heat and simmer until the sweet potatoes are nearly tender, 5 to 8 minutes.

2. Add the black beans, tomatoes, bouillon cubes, scallions, salsa, chili powder, and 2 cups of additional water. Return to a slow boil, then lower the heat, cover, and simmer for 10 minutes longer.

3. Season with salt and pepper. Stir in the spinach and cook briefly, just until it wilts. Remove from the heat, stir in the cilantro, and serve.

NOTE

To make the sweet potatoes easier to peel, microwave them until they're about half done. You should be able to pierce them, but with a lot of resistance. When they're cool enough to handle, peel and dice them. This can be done ahead of time.

Broccoli Cheddar Soup

6 servings

If your household members like broccoli, they'll be sure to enjoy this soothing classic with a cheesy spin. This is a great soup to serve with just about any kind of wraps or sandwiches. See some sandwich recipe ideas on pages 100 to 108, or serve with any of your favorites.

1 tablespoon olive oil

1 large onion, chopped

2 vegetable bouillon cubes

2 teaspoons salt-free seasoning (for more information, see page xxiii)

8 cups chopped broccoli florets

1 cup frozen green peas, thawed

1 (15-ounce) can Great Northern or cannellini beans, drained and rinsed

1 cup unsweetened nondairy milk, plus more as needed

1½ cups vegan cheddar shreds

2 tablespoons lemon juice (fresh or bottled), or more to taste

Salt and freshly ground pepper, to taste

1. Heat the oil in a soup pot. Add the onions and sauté over medium heat until golden.

2. Add 4 cups of water, the bouillon cubes, the salt-free seasoning, and 6 cups of the broccoli (set aside the remainder to finish the soup). Bring to a slow boil, then lower the heat, cover, and simmer gently until the broccoli is tender but not overcooked, about 8 to 10 minutes.

3. Add the peas and beans. Continue to simmer just until everything is nicely heated through.

4. The easiest way to puree this soup is to simply insert an immersion blender into the pot and puree until it's as smooth as you'd like, or leave it a bit chunky. (Or, transfer the mixture, in batches, to a regular blender and puree—don't overprocess—then transfer back to the soup pot.) Stir in enough nondairy milk to give the soup a medium-thick consistency.

5. To finish the soup, finely chop the remaining broccoli florets. Add them to the soup, along with the cheese shreds and lemon juice, and stir until the cheese is melted.

6. Season with salt and pepper, then cook over low heat for 5 minutes longer, or until the broccoli florets are tender-crisp. Serve at once.

Vegan on a Budget

Italian Pasta & Bean Soup

6 to 8 servings

Pasta e Fagioli, a classic Italian soup that's a cousin to minestrone, is another hearty main dish in a bowl. Serve with a crusty bread and a simple salad or a platter of raw vegetables with an easy dip, like Tartar Dressing or Dip (page 199).

2 tablespoons olive oil

1 medium onion, finely chopped

2 cloves garlic, minced

3 large celery stalks, diced

3 medium carrots, peeled and sliced

1 (28-ounce) can diced tomatoes, preferably fire-roasted or Italian-style

2 vegetable bouillon cubes

2 teaspoons Italian seasoning

2 heaping cups (uncooked) pasta (any short shape)

2 (15-ounce) cans cannellini or pink beans, drained and rinsed, or 3 cups cooked beans

Salt and freshly ground pepper, to taste

¼ to ½ cup chopped fresh parsley

1. Heat the oil in a large soup pot. Add the onions and sauté over medium heat until translucent. Add the garlic and celery, and continue to sauté until all are golden.

2. Add the carrots, tomatoes, bouillon cubes, Italian seasoning, and 6 cups of water. Bring to a slow boil, then lower the heat, cover, and simmer gently for 20 minutes.

3. Meanwhile, cook the pasta according to the package directions in a separate saucepan until al dente, then drain.

4. When the broth mixture has simmered for 20 minutes, add the cooked pasta, along with the beans, and simmer gently for 5 minutes longer.

5. Adjust the consistency with a little more water if the soup is too crowded. Season with salt and pepper, stir in the parsley, and serve.

Tortilla Soup with Summer Squash & Corn

6 servings

There are lots of ways to make and serve this classic Southwestern soup, but this is my favorite. I like to toast strips of the tortillas and use them either as a base for the finished soup or as a garnish. Either way, the crisp corn tortillas add a major yum factor. This soup can be enjoyed any time of year, though it's especially good in late summer and early fall when squash and fresh corn are abundant. Though the ingredients list looks a bit long, it's easy to make at a relaxing pace and doesn't need much cooking time.

1 tablespoon olive oil

1 large onion, chopped

2 to 3 cloves garlic, minced

1 medium bell pepper (any color), finely diced

2 medium zucchini or yellow squash (or 1 of each), diced

1 (15-ounce) can diced tomatoes, preferably fire-roasted

1 (15-ounce) can tomato sauce

2 cups fresh or frozen (thawed) corn kernels

1 or 2 fresh hot chiles, seeded and chopped

2 teaspoons ground cumin

2 teaspoons salt-free seasoning (for more information, see page xxiii)

¼ to ½ cup chopped fresh cilantro plus more for garnish

Salt and freshly ground pepper, to taste

FOR THE GARNISH

6 corn tortillas or about 12 mini tortillas

1 medium firm ripe avocado, peeled and sliced, optional

1. Heat the oil in a large soup pot. Add the onions and garlic, and sauté over medium heat until golden.

2. Add 5 cups of water, plus all the remaining ingredients except for the cilantro and salt and pepper. Bring to a slow boil, then lower the heat, cover, and simmer gently for 10 minutes.

3. Stir in a little more water if the soup is too crowded. Stir in the cilantro and season with salt and pepper.

4. While the soup is cooking, cut the tortillas into 2- by ¼-inch strips. Spray a large skillet with a little cooking oil spray or coat it with a little olive oil and heat it over medium-high heat until hot. Add the tortilla strips and toast them, turning frequently, until dry and crisp, then transfer them to a plate to cool.

5. Once the soup is done, garnish each serving with some tortilla strips, extra cilantro, and a few slices of avocado, if desired.

VARIATION

■ To make this a main dish soup, add about 3 cups of cooked
black or pinto beans, or two 15-ounce cans, drained and rinsed.

Creamy Mushroom Soup
with Hearty Grains

8 or more servings

Taking the classic mushroom-barley combination a step further by offering the option of using a different whole grain and incorporating hardy greens, this is one very substantial, nourishing soup. The addition of pureed tofu or white beans ensures creamy comfort, too. Keep this recipe in mind for a chilly or rainy day.

1 cup uncooked barley or other whole grain (see Variations)

2 tablespoons olive oil

1 large or 2 medium onions, chopped (or see Variations)

3 to 4 cloves garlic, chopped

2 vegetable bouillon cubes

1 (14-ounce) tub soft tofu, or 15-ounce can cannellini beans, drained and rinsed

2 cups unsweetened nondairy milk, plus more as needed

8 ounces cremini (baby bella) mushrooms, cleaned, stemmed, and sliced

2 cups stemmed and finely chopped greens (kale, collards, or chard)

¼ cup finely chopped fresh parsley

2 tablespoons minced fresh dill (or 1 teaspoon dried)

Salt and freshly ground pepper, to taste

1. If you're using barley, combine it with 3 cups of water in a large saucepan and bring it to a slow boil. Lower the heat, cover, and simmer until the water is absorbed, 35 to 40 minutes, or until done to your liking. If you're using another grain, see Variations for water amounts and cooking times. Once all the water is absorbed, remove from the heat and set aside.

2. Heat the oil in a large soup pot. Add the onions and garlic, and cook over medium heat, stirring occasionally, until golden.

3. Add the bouillon cubes and 2 cups of water. Bring to a slow boil, then lower the heat and simmer gently for 10 minutes.

4. Transfer about half of the solids from the soup pot to a blender or a large food processor. Add the tofu or beans and 2 cups of the nondairy milk, then process until the mixture is velvety smooth. Transfer to the soup pot and stir in with the remaining solids. (Or, simply add the tofu or beans and the nondairy milk to the soup pot, insert an immersion blender into the soup, and process until about half of the solids are pureed.)

5. Add the mushrooms. Return to a simmer and cook until the mushrooms are tender, about 15 minutes longer.

6. Add the chopped greens and the reserved cooked grain. Simmer for 15 minutes longer, or until the greens are tender but still retain their color.

7. Stir in the chopped parsley and dill, then stir in more water or nondairy milk, if needed to give the soup a medium-thick consistency. Simmer the soup for 5 minutes longer, or until heated through. Season with salt and pepper and serve.

NOTE

This soup thickens substantially as it stands. Thin with more water and/or nondairy milk, and adjust seasonings as needed.

VARIATIONS

For the grain, you can go with the classic barley, but this soup is also good with quinoa, brown rice, or farro. To use these alternate grains, follow step 1 in the recipe, using the following water amounts and cooking times:

- For 1 cup quinoa, use 2 cups water and simmer for 15 minutes.
- For 1 cup brown rice, use 2½ cups water and simmer for 30 minutes.
- For 1 cup farro, use 3 cups water and simmer for 35 to 40 minutes.

This step can be done ahead of time.

Use 2 large or 3 medium leeks in place of the onion in step 2 for a lovely effect. First, remove and discard the stem ends and the coarse green leaves. Using the white and the palest green parts only, cut each leek in half lengthwise, and then slice into half circles. Place in a colander and rinse well, using your hands to separate the rings and make sure that no grit remains.

VARIATION

Instead of using all carrots, use a 16-ounce bag of baby carrots plus a 16-ounce bag of fresh parsnips. It's debatable whether parsnips need to be peeled. If they're small and look very fresh, you can get away with scrubbing them well (especially if you'll be pureeing this in a blender, rather than using an immersion blender). If the parsnips are larger and tougher, go that extra step and peel them. In any event, you'll need to cut the parsnips into small pieces, similar in size to the baby carrots, so they can be cooked together at the same time.

Carrot Ginger Soup

6 to 8 servings

A carrot puree offers concentrated nourishment and a burst of comforting color in a bowl. Let's face it, though—peeling and chopping two pounds of carrots is a bit of a project. A quicker route to this brilliant-hued soup is provided by two bags of baby carrots. Try replacing half the carrots with parsnips, another economical cool-weather vegetable (see Variation).

1 tablespoon olive oil

1 large onion, chopped

2 to 3 cloves garlic, minced

2 (16-ounce) bags baby carrots (or see Variation)

1 (15-ounce) can diced tomatoes, preferably fire-roasted

2 to 3 teaspoons grated fresh or squeeze-bottle ginger

1½ to 2 cups nondairy milk, or as needed (for more information, see page xix)

Zest and juice of 1 orange

Salt and freshly ground pepper, to taste

Chopped fresh parsley or cilantro for garnish, optional

1. Heat the oil in a soup pot. Add the onions and sauté over low heat until translucent. Add the garlic and continue to sauté until both are golden.

2. Add the carrots, tomatoes, and ginger, along with enough water to not quite cover the vegetables. Bring to a slow boil, then reduce the heat, cover, and simmer gently until the carrots are tender, about 20 to 30 minutes, depending on their thickness. Remove from the heat.

3. With a slotted spoon, transfer the cooked vegetables, along with a little of the cooking liquid, in batches, to a blender. Blend (use caution when blending hot liquids) to a smooth consistency and return the puree to the soup pot. (Or, simply insert an immersion blender into the soup pot and process until smooth, unless you prefer a little texture.)

4. Stir in enough nondairy milk to give the soup a medium-thick consistency.

5. Return to low heat. Add the orange zest and juice, then season with salt and pepper. Sprinkle each serving with parsley or cilantro, if desired, and serve at once.

Smoky Red Lentil Soup
with Mushroom Bacon

8 or more servings

This dense, warming soup is a natural choice as a hearty main dish. Not only does it come together in a relatively short time, it yields bonus servings because it thickens so much as it stands. While it very much resembles a yellow split pea soup, tiny red lentils take a fraction of the time to cook. Red lentils can be bought in bulk, or sometimes you'll find them in the supermarket in 16-ounce bags, shelved with other dry legumes. In a pinch, you can skip the mushroom bacon, but it's really what gives this soup its wow factor.

2 tablespoons olive oil

1 cup finely chopped onion

2 medium carrots, peeled and diced

2 to 3 cloves garlic, crushed or minced

2 vegetable bouillon cubes

16 ounces red lentils, rinsed

2 teaspoons good-quality curry powder, or to taste

2 teaspoons barbecue seasoning, or to taste (for more information, see page xxii)

2 teaspoons grated fresh or squeeze-bottle ginger

Mushroom Bacon (page 195)

Salt and freshly ground pepper, to taste

Chopped fresh parsley or cilantro for topping, optional

1. Heat the oil in a soup pot. Add the onions and sauté over medium-low heat until golden.

2. Add the carrots, garlic, bouillon cubes, 8 cups of water (or see Variation), lentils, curry powder, barbecue seasoning, and ginger. Bring to a slow boil, then lower the heat, cover, and simmer gently, stirring occasionally, until the lentils are mushy, about 20 minutes.

3. Meanwhile, make the Mushroom Bacon. Set aside and cover until needed.

4. When the lentils are done, stir in a little more water, as needed, to give the soup a medium-thick consistency, then season with salt and pepper. (This soup thickens considerably as it stands; thin with additional water as needed and adjust the seasonings.)

5. Top each serving with some of the Mushroom Bacon and the parsley, if using, and serve.

VARIATION

■ Replace 2 cups of the water with a 14-ounce can of light coconut milk for a subtle yet luscious layer of flavor and aroma.

Two-Potato Soup

6 servings

Combining golden and sweet potatoes in a soup is my idea of pure comfort and joy, but peeling and dicing six to eight potatoes gives me pause. So I've made the process easier by microwaving the potatoes first so that the skins easily slip off and the chopping is then a breeze.

2 large or 3 medium sweet potatoes

6 medium or 4 large golden potatoes

1 tablespoon olive oil

1 large yellow onion, chopped

2 vegetable bouillon cubes

2 to 3 cups unsweetened nondairy milk, or as needed

2 teaspoons yellow mustard

1 cup vegan cheddar shreds, optional

Salt and freshly ground pepper, to taste

¼ to ½ cup chopped fresh parsley

¼ cup chopped fresh dill, optional

1. Microwave the sweet potatoes until easily pierced with a knife. Do the same with the golden potatoes. Set the potatoes aside until they're cool enough to handle. (You can speed up the cooling process by immersing the potatoes in a bowl of ice water.)

2. Heat the oil in a soup pot. Add the onions and sauté over medium-low heat until lightly browned.

3. Add 2 cups of water, plus the bouillon cubes, and bring to a slow boil, then turn down to a simmer.

4. Once the potatoes are cool enough to handle, slip the skins off and cut them into large chunks. Add them to the soup pot and stir to combine. Using a potato masher, mash the potatoes in the pot as much as you'd like, leaving some chunks for texture.

5. Stir in enough nondairy milk to give the soup a fluid but fairly thick consistency. Stir in the mustard and cheddar shreds, if using, and return to a simmer. Cook for 10 minutes longer.

6. While the soup is simmering, if you are using the Spiced Chickpeas or Tempeh Bacon or the prepared tempeh bacon as a topping, prepare them now (see Optional Additions).

7. Season the soup with salt and pepper. Top each bowlful with the parsley and the dill, if using, along with the Optional Additions, if desired. Serve at once.

OPTIONAL ADDITIONS

- Add protein to the soup with a topping of Spiced Chickpeas (page 145), Tempeh Bacon (page 196), or a 6- to 8-ounce package of prepared tempeh bacon. Tempeh bacon, homemade or not, should be cut into small bits to use as a topping.

About Bouillon Cubes
& Other Soup Flavoring Options

You'll notice that many of the recipes in this chapter call for bouillon cubes. Depending on their size, one or two vegetable bouillon cubes add significant flavor to a soup's base, and they're a far less costly option than using a ready-made quart of vegetable broth.

Read the labels carefully and look for a no-salt-added brand with all-natural ingredients. My favorite is Rapunzel Vegan Vegetable Bouillon; each cube is equivalent to two standard-sized cubes.

Other excellent options are vegetable broth powder and vegetable bouillon base. They come close to bouillon cubes in terms of economy. Once again, check labels carefully to make sure they're vegan, that they contain all-natural ingredients, and don't have a crazy amount of sodium. Rapunzel also makes a good vegetable broth powder, and the best-known brand of vegetable bouillon base is Better Than Bouillon.

Overall, because they're so readily available, bouillon cubes are the easiest to find and the most economical option in this category. Plus, you can choose a salt-free variety if you prefer.

Tomato, Barley & Vegetable Soup

8 or more servings

Featuring frugal ingredients like potatoes, carrots, onions, and celery, this soup is nothing fancy, but it's immensely satisfying. It's also quite filling, so plan for it to be the centerpiece of a meal. How about serving it with vegan grilled cheese sandwiches? This is an embellished version of tomato soup, after all, and that's a classic duo.

2 tablespoons olive oil

1 large or 2 medium onions, finely chopped

2 cloves garlic, minced, optional

2 celery stalks, thinly sliced, with leaves

1 cup pearl barley, rinsed

3 medium carrots, peeled and sliced

1 large potato, scrubbed, if organic; (otherwise peeled) and diced

2 teaspoons salt-free seasoning (for more information, see page xxiii)

2 teaspoons sweet paprika

1 (28-ounce) can crushed tomatoes

Salt and freshly ground pepper, to taste

¼ cup chopped fresh dill, plus more for garnish

1. Heat the oil in a large soup pot. Add the onions and sauté over low heat until golden.

2. Add the garlic, celery, barley, carrots, potato, salt-free seasoning, paprika, and 8 cups of water. Bring to a slow boil, then lower the heat, cover, and simmer gently, stirring occasionally, for 30 minutes. The barley and vegetables should be nearly done.

3. Add the tomatoes and continue to simmer for 15 to 20 minutes, or until the barley and vegetables are tender.

4. Stir in a little more water, if necessary, and season with salt and pepper. Stir in the dill and serve, garnished with more dill.

NOTE

This soup thickens considerably as it stands, especially if it's refrigerated to be used as leftovers. Adjust the liquid and seasonings as needed, but allow the soup to remain thick.

French-Style Onion Soup

6 servings

Here's a vegan rendition of the French classic, complete with crusty bread and melted cheese. Though there's a fair amount of onion-cutting (and, likely, shedding of tears), quartering and slicing them is easy. It takes some time to cook the onions slowly, but your patience will be rewarded. You'll need heatproof bowls for finishing this soup in the oven; any kind of sturdy ovenproof bowls will do.

2 tablespoons olive oil

6 large or 8 medium yellow or red onions, quartered and thinly sliced

2 to 4 cloves garlic, minced

2 vegetable bouillon cubes

Salt and freshly ground pepper, to taste

Long, narrow French or Italian bread, as needed

1½ cups vegan mozzarella-style shreds

1. Heat the oil in a soup pot. Add the onions and sauté over medium-low heat until golden. Add the garlic and continue to sauté slowly, stirring frequently, until the onions are lightly and evenly browned, 20 to 30 minutes.

2. Stir in 6 cups of water and the bouillon cubes. Bring to a slow boil, then lower the heat, cover, and simmer gently for 15 minutes. Season with salt and pepper.

3. Preheat the oven to 375°F and place 6 heatproof bowls on 1 or 2 sturdy baking sheets for easy handling.

4. Cut the bread into 1-inch-thick slices, allowing 1 or 2 slices per serving, depending on the size of your soup bowls. Arrange the slices on a baking sheet and bake for 15 minutes, or until dry and crisp, flipping the slices over once about halfway through the baking time.

5. Distribute the soup among the soup bowls. Place 1 or 2 slices of the bread on top of the soup in each bowl, depending on the size of the slices and the width of the bowls. Finish with a sprinkling of ¼ cup of the cheese shreds, mainly over the bread.

6. Bake for about 10 minutes, or until the cheese is melted. Serve at once.

Asian Noodle Soup
with Lettuce & Mushrooms

4 to 6 servings

This simple noodle soup is a good introduction to a simple stir-fry or tofu dish. Try it with Tofu, Bok Choy & Baby Corn Teriyaki (page 52). Rice noodles (sometimes called rice vermicelli) and bean thread noodles are no longer exotic items that you have to go hunting for. You'll find them in the Asian foods section of well-stocked supermarkets, and they're a bargain.

1 (4-ounce) bundle rice noodles or bean thread noodles (or see Variations)

2 vegetable bouillon cubes

8 ounces cremini (baby bella) mushrooms, cleaned, stemmed, and sliced

2 teaspoons grated fresh or squeeze-bottle ginger

½ head romaine lettuce, thinly shredded

2 to 3 scallions, thinly sliced

2 tablespoons soy sauce or tamari, or to taste

Freshly ground black pepper, to taste

1. Cook the noodles according to the package directions. Drain well, then transfer them to a cutting board and chop in several directions with a knife or kitchen shears to shorten.

2. Meanwhile, combine 4 cups of water, the bouillon cubes, mushrooms, and ginger in a soup pot. Bring to a slow boil, then lower the heat, cover, and simmer gently for 10 minutes.

3. Add the lettuce, scallions, and soy sauce and simmer for 2 to 3 minutes, just until the lettuce is wilted, but slightly crunchy.

4. Stir in the cooked noodles and add a little more water if the soup is too crowded.

5. Season with pepper, then add more soy sauce, if needed. Serve at once.

VARIATIONS

- Substitute any ordinary thin pasta, like angel hair or thin spaghetti, for the Asian noodles. Ramen noodles work just as well—a 5-ounce package is perfect for this soup. With any of these variations, cook the noodles according to the package instructions.

- Drop in a couple of big handfuls of baby spinach when adding the lettuce.

Asian-Style Vegetable & Tofu Soup

4 to 6 servings

This colorful soup can be on your table in less time than it would take to order and pick up a similar soup from your local Chinese eatery. Serve with an Asian-flavored noodle dish for a fun meal. Might I suggest Vegetable Chow Mein (page 95)?

2 vegetable bouillon cubes

1 (15-ounce) can cut baby corn, with liquid

2 teaspoons grated fresh or squeeze-bottle ginger

2 cups small broccoli florets

1 cup grated carrots (DIY or packaged)

¾ cup frozen (thawed) peas or trimmed fresh snow peas

1 (14-ounce) tub firm or extra-firm tofu

2 scallions, thinly sliced

Soy sauce or tamari, to taste

Freshly ground pepper, to taste

1. Combine 4 cups of water, the bouillon cubes, baby corn with liquid, and ginger in a soup pot and bring to a simmer.

2. Add the broccoli, carrots, and peas. If the vegetables are too crowded, stir in another ½ to 1 cup of water.

3. Cut the tofu into 8 slabs, then cut into small dice. Add the tofu cubes to the soup, along with the scallions, and return the soup to a rapid simmer.

4. Season with soy sauce and pepper. Cover and let stand off the heat for 5 minutes, then serve.

Seitan & Vegetable Stew

6 to 8 servings

High-protein seitan gives this stew a truly meaty texture. Prepared seitan is readily available in most natural foods stores, as well as a growing number of well-stocked supermarkets. But for real economy, see the recipe on page 192 for making your own Homemade Seitan. A simple coleslaw is all you need to complete the meal; see ideas under Simple Slaws (page 137).

2 tablespoons olive oil, divided

1 large onion, quartered and thinly sliced

2 cloves garlic, minced

5 medium potatoes, peeled and diced

4 medium carrots, peeled and sliced

2 cups fresh green beans, cut into 1-inch lengths, or frozen cut green beans

1 vegetable bouillon cube

2 teaspoons salt-free seasoning (for more information, see page xxiii)

1 to 1½ pounds seitan or Homemade Seitan (page 192), cut into bite-sized pieces

Salt and freshly ground pepper, to taste

Chopped fresh parsley for garnish, optional

1. Heat 1 tablespoon of olive oil in a large soup pot. Add the onions and garlic, and sauté over medium heat until the onions are golden.

2. Add 3 cups of water, along with the potatoes, carrots, green beans, bouillon cube, and salt-free seasoning. Bring to a slow boil, then lower the heat, cover, and simmer gently for 25 to 30 minutes, or until the potatoes and carrots are tender.

3. Meanwhile, heat the remaining tablespoon of oil in a large skillet. Add the seitan and sauté over medium-high heat, stirring frequently, until most sides are nicely browned.

4. Once the vegetables are done, use the back of a wooden spoon to mash enough of the potatoes to thicken the base of the stew.

5. Stir the sautéed seitan into the stew, then stir in a little more water, if necessary, to give the soup a thick and moist (but not soupy) consistency.

6. Season with salt and pepper and serve in shallow bowls. Pass around the parsley for garnishing individual portions, if using.

Ramen Noodle Vegetable Soup

4 to 6 servings

There are times when you need a hot, soothing soup, and you need it immediately. Perhaps you've just arrived home on a chilly day, exhausted, or you're coming down with something and the last thing you feel like doing is standing and chopping. That's when this super-easy soup comes in handy.

The clever shortcut here is a bag of frozen mixed Asian vegetables. They taste surprisingly fresh, and stay nice and crisp in the soup, if you're careful not to overcook them. Ramen noodles are now readily available (without the soup mix) in the Asian foods section of well-stocked supermarkets, sometimes labeled *chuka soba*.

2 vegetable bouillon cubes

1 (5-ounce) package curly ramen noodles (*chuka soba*)

1 16-ounce bag frozen mixed Asian vegetables

2 teaspoons grated fresh or squeeze-bottle ginger

7 to 8 ounces firm or extra-firm tofu (about half of a 14-ounce tub), diced

2 scallions, thinly sliced

2 big handfuls baby spinach or other baby greens

2 tablespoons soy sauce, or to taste

Freshly ground pepper, to taste

Sriracha or another hot sauce, optional

1. Combine 6 cups of water and the bouillon cubes in a small soup pot and bring to a slow boil.

2. Add the ramen noodles, Asian vegetables, and ginger. Return to a slow boil, then lower the heat and simmer until the noodles are al dente. (The vegetables will be just done at this point as well.)

3. Reach into the pot with a pair of kitchen shears and cut the noodles here and there (they're very long!). Stir in a little more water if the soup is too crowded.

4. Add the tofu, scallions, and greens and continue to simmer until the greens are just wilted and everything is heated through.

5. Season with soy sauce and pepper. If you'd like a spicier soup, add sriracha or another hot sauce to taste, or, better yet, pass the hot sauce around at the table. Serve at once.

NOTE

The noodles absorb the broth as it stands. Add more water as needed and adjust the seasonings.

Vegan on a Budget

White Bean Chili
with Sweet Potatoes & Squash

6 to 8 servings

Here's a warming cool-weather stew that comes together quickly, thanks to the salsa, which adds plenty of flavor without a lot of extra ingredients. And, instead of the usual chili powder, a barbecue seasoning blend offers even more depth of flavor. Just add fresh bread and a simple green salad for a satisfying meal.

1 tablespoon olive oil

1 large onion, finely chopped

2 to 3 cloves garlic, minced

1 large sweet potato, peeled and diced

1 (28-ounce) can cannellini or Great Northern beans (or two 15-ounce cans), drained and rinsed

1 (15-ounce) can small red or kidney beans, drained and rinsed

1 (15-ounce) can diced tomatoes, preferably fire-roasted

1 cup salsa (any variety)

1 tablespoon barbecue seasoning (for more information, see page xxii)

2 teaspoons ground cumin

1 medium yellow summer squash

1 or 2 hot chili peppers, such as jalapeño, optional

Salt and freshly ground pepper, to taste

Fresh cilantro or parsley leaves or sprigs of oregano, for garnish, optional

1. Heat the oil in a soup pot. Add the onions and sauté over medium heat until translucent. Add the garlic and continue to sauté until the onions are golden.

2. Add the sweet potatoes and 2 cups of water. Bring to a slow boil, then lower the heat, cover, and simmer for 5 minutes.

3. Add both types of beans, tomatoes, salsa, barbecue seasoning, and cumin, and return to a simmer.

4. Cut the squash in half lengthwise. Slice the thinner end into half-circles; cut each half of the thicker end in half again and slice. Add to the soup pot, along with the optional chili peppers.

5. Return to a simmer and cook, covered, until the squash and sweet potatoes are tender but not overcooked, about 10 minutes.

6. Stir in a little more water if the stew is too dense, but let it stay nice and thick. Season with salt and pepper. If time allows, let the stew stand off the heat for 30 minutes to an hour to develop flavor, then heat through as needed. But if you can't wait, by all means, serve at once.

7. Garnish each serving with fresh herbs of your choice, if desired.

Quick Lentil
& Kidney Bean Curry

4 to 6 servings

Inspired by an Indian recipe that combines two tasty high-protein legumes, this lentil and kidney bean curry makes a quick, filling main-dish stew. The traditional recipe uses 15 to 20 ingredients, many of which are spices. For this nearly instant version, you'll be using one of several vegan varieties of ready-made Indian simmer sauces, a shortcut I recommend throughout this book.

Serve with rice or another grain and/or a flatbread. Naan is a real treat, or you can opt for pita bread if it's fresh. I happened to have some cooked black rice (also known as forbidden rice) on hand for the accompanying photo, but you can use any rice or another grain—or skip the grain altogether.

1 tablespoon olive oil

1 medium onion, finely chopped

2 to 3 cloves garlic, minced

1 medium tomato, diced

1 (10- to 12-ounce) jar Indian simmer sauce (see Note)

3 cups cooked brown lentils or two 15-ounce cans, drained and rinsed

1 (15-ounce) can kidney beans, drained and rinsed

1 tablespoon lemon or lime juice

¼ cup chopped fresh cilantro

Salt and freshly ground pepper, to taste

1. Heat the oil in a small soup pot or steep-sided stir-fry pan. Add the onions and sauté over medium heat until translucent. Add the garlic and continue to sauté until the onions are golden.

2. Add the tomatoes, Indian simmer sauce, lentils, kidney beans, and lemon juice. Turn the heat up and bring to a simmer, then lower it and cook over low heat for 5 to 8 minutes, or until piping hot. Stir occasionally.

3. Stir in the cilantro, season with salt (you may not need any salt at all, so taste first) and pepper, and serve.

NOTE

Look for Indian simmer sauces in the international foods aisles in supermarkets and in natural foods stores. They come in a range of vegan options from mild to spicy, including Goan coconut, Kashmir curry, Jalfrezi, and Madras curry. Some include dairy, so be sure to check the labels.

VARIATION

- Sauté 2 links of vegan sausage (cut ½ inch thick) or about a cup of vegan chorizo in a small skillet until lightly browned, then add to the stew in step 3.

Spanish-Style Chickpea Stew

6 to 8 servings

A chickpea stew in a thick tomatoey, paprika-scented base is my take on a classic Spanish recipe. Sometimes spinach is added, sometimes not; sometimes it's an already vegan dish, while other times some chorizo is added. Feel free to use vegan sausage or vegan chorizo, as suggested in the Variation, though I find it hearty enough in its simple form.

This makes a nice meal served over rice or quinoa (or, as shown in the photo, a combination of white rice and red quinoa—the two grains can be cooked together) or on its own. Complete the meal with a simple green salad or slaw, and, if you're serving it without a grain, you can add fresh bread as well.

1½ tablespoons olive oil

1 large onion, chopped

3 to 4 cloves garlic, minced

1 large green bell pepper, cut into short, slender strips

1 (28-ounce) can chickpeas, drained and rinsed

1 (28-ounce) can diced tomatoes, preferably fire-roasted

1 teaspoon ground cumin

1 teaspoon dried oregano

1 to 2 teaspoons smoked or sweet paprika, to taste

¼ cup chopped fresh parsley or cilantro, plus more for garnish

Salt and freshly ground pepper, to taste

Hot cooked rice or another grain, optional

1. Heat the oil in a large soup pot. Add the onions and sauté over medium-low heat until translucent. Add the garlic and green pepper, and continue to sauté until all are touched with golden spots.

2. Add the chickpeas, tomatoes, cumin, oregano, paprika, and 1½ cups water. Bring to a slow boil, then lower the heat, cover, and simmer gently for 15 minutes.

3. Stir in the parsley or cilantro and season with salt and pepper.

4. Serve in bowls on its own or over a small amount of hot cooked rice or another grain, if desired. Pass around some extra parsley or cilantro for garnishing each serving.

West African–Inspired Peanut Stew

6 to 8 servings

This is a Westernized version of a classic African stew, made in various ways across the continent. I discovered it when my kids were in elementary school. Because I had a reputation as a "food mom," I was assigned to organize the preparation of it for a class on African cultures. I thought there was no way the kids would eat it, especially with the okra, but I was proven wrong. They cleaned every last drop from the very large pots we used, and I've been making it at home ever since. What gives this stew its luscious flavor is a peanut butter–flavored base.

1½ tablespoons olive oil

1 large yellow or red onion, chopped

3 to 4 cloves garlic, minced

3 cups shredded white cabbage

2 large sweet potatoes, peeled and cut into ½-inch dice

1 (14-ounce) can diced tomatoes, preferably fire-roasted

1 tablespoon grated fresh or squeeze-bottle ginger, or to taste

8 to 10 ounces fresh okra or 10-ounce package frozen sliced okra, thawed (see Variation)

½ cup natural creamy peanut butter

Salt and freshly ground pepper, to taste

Dried hot red pepper flakes or sriracha, to taste

Sliced scallions for garnish, optional

Chopped peanuts for garnish, optional

1. Heat the oil in a soup pot. Add the onions and garlic, and sauté over medium heat until the onions are golden.

2. Add the cabbage, sweet potatoes, tomatoes, ginger, and 3 cups of water. Bring to a slow boil, then lower the heat and simmer gently, covered, until the sweet potatoes and the cabbage are nearly tender, about 10 minutes.

3. Add the okra, then stir in the peanut butter, a little at a time, until it melts into the broth. Simmer gently, covered, for 10 minutes longer, or until all the vegetables are tender. Stir in a little more water, if necessary, to give the stew a moist (but not soupy) consistency.

4. Season with salt and pepper, then add enough of the hot seasoning to your liking (or you can pass the red pepper flakes or sriracha around the table). Garnish each serving with the sliced scallions and/or chopped peanuts, if desired.

VARIATION

■ Okra may not be everyone's favorite vegetable, but in this dish, as the characteristic ingredient, it's very good. However, if you're not a fan, substitute a 10-ounce package of frozen cut green beans (or fresh green beans, if they're in season—about 2 cups green beans cut into 2-inch lengths) for results that are equally delectable, if a bit less authentic.

2

A FRESH FLASH IN THE PAN: SKILLETS & STIR-FRIES

Here's a selection of good-for-you dishes, made on the stovetop, that are based on plant-based staples—beans, rice, quinoa, and tofu (with a brief nod to seitan and vegan sausage). These skillets and stir-fries are filled with wholesome ingredients, yet still manage to fulfill that desire for coziness and comfort that we all crave at the end of the day. With these one-dish meals, all that's needed is something fresh and raw to brighten the plate (or bowl)—a simple salad or a platter of veggies—and dinner is served.

Indian-Spiced Cauliflower & Chickpeas

6 to 8 servings

My family loves Indian food but, even at modest-priced eateries, an in-house or take-out meal of four modest-portion main dishes and samosas can add up. On the other hand, a meal centered around this delectable cauliflower and chickpea recipe, even with an optional splurge of frozen samosas, is much more affordable.

I'm too lazy to roast and grind and mix and measure the myriad spices that give Indian-style dishes their amazing flavors, so this dish relies on the kind of Indian simmer sauces I've come to love. Serve the curry alone in shallow bowls or over hot cooked grains. To turn this dish into a stew, just add coconut milk (see Variations).

---

1 tablespoon olive oil

1 medium onion, finely chopped

2 cloves garlic, minced

2 (16-ounce) bags frozen cauliflower florets, thawed (see Notes)

1 (28-ounce) can chickpeas, drained and rinsed

3 medium ripe juicy tomatoes, chopped

1 (12- to 16-ounce) jar Indian simmer sauce (see Notes)

1 teaspoon curry powder (for color)

2 teaspoons minced fresh or squeeze-bottle ginger

Salt and freshly ground pepper, to taste

¼ cup chopped fresh cilantro or sliced basil leaves, or to taste

Hot cooked rice or another grain, to serve (optional)

1. Heat the oil in a large soup pot. Add the onions and sauté over medium heat until translucent. Add the garlic and continue to sauté until both are golden, about 5 minutes

2. Add the cauliflower, chickpeas, tomatoes, Indian simmer sauce, and about ½ cup of water. Stir in the curry powder and ginger.

3. Bring the mixture to a slow boil, then lower the heat, cover, and simmer over medium-low heat for 5 to 8 minutes, until everything is piping hot.

4. Season with salt and pepper. Stir in the cilantro or basil and serve at once in shallow bowls on its own, or over hot cooked grains, if desired.

NOTES

Though using frozen cauliflower makes this dish easier to tackle at the end the day, you're certainly free to use fresh. You'll need one large head, cut into bite-sized florets. Steam until tender-crisp before adding to the dish.

Look for Indian simmer sauces in the international foods aisles in supermarkets and in natural foods stores. They come in a range of vegan options from mild to spicy, including Goan coconut, Kashmir curry, Jalfrezi, and Madras curry. Some include dairy, so be sure to check labels.

VARIATIONS

- Use a 15-ounce can of diced tomatoes if good fresh tomatoes aren't available.
- To make this dish more like a stew, add a 15-ounce can of light coconut milk in step 2. Or, add the coconut milk to leftovers to stretch the recipe.

OPTIONAL ADDITIONS

- If you're a garlic fan, add 3 to 4 cloves of minced garlic when the onions are translucent, then continue as directed.
- Drop in 4 to 5 stemmed and sliced kale leaves for added color and nutrition when adding the cabbage.

Vegan Sausage Skillet with Cabbage & Potatoes

4 to 6 servings

There are few vegetables that give you more bang for the buck than cabbage and potatoes. Transforming a classic sausage and cabbage skillet into a plant-based version is easy to do with vegan sausage, and adding potatoes to the mix makes it much more substantial.

Serve this with a simple tossed salad and add a steamed green vegetable if you'd like—green beans or broccoli go especially well with this dish.

---

4 medium red-skinned or golden potatoes, scrubbed

1 large or 2 medium onions, quartered and sliced

½ large head cabbage, thinly sliced, or 16-ounce bag coleslaw

1 (14-ounce) package (4 links) vegan sausage, cut into ½-inch slices

2 tablespoons olive oil, divided

¼ cup white wine or water

¼ to ½ cup chopped fresh parsley

Salt and freshly ground pepper, to taste

Dried hot red pepper flakes, to taste (optional)

1. Microwave the potatoes all at once until they're about half done—you should be able to pierce them, but get some resistance. Start with 4 minutes, and add another minute as needed. Plunge them into a bowl of cold water and let them stand for about 10 minutes.

2. While the potatoes are cooling, prepare the onions, cabbage, and sausage as directed.

3. When the potatoes are cool enough to handle, cut them into bite-sized chunks. Heat 1 tablespoon of the oil in a large skillet or stir-fry pan. Add the potatoes and sausage and sauté over medium-high heat, stirring often, until they're turning golden here and there, about 10 minutes. Transfer to a plate or bowl and set aside.

4. Heat the remaining tablespoon of oil in the same pan. Add the onions and sauté over medium heat until golden. Add the cabbage and wine or water, cover, and cook until wilted down, about 5 minutes. Uncover, turn the heat up to medium-high, and cook, stirring often, for 5 minutes longer.

5. Return the sausage and potato mixture to the pan and stir together with the cabbage and onions. Stir in the parsley. Season with salt, pepper, and the red pepper flakes, if using. Sauté for 5 minutes longer, then serve.

Barbecue-Flavored White Beans with Sausage & Spinach

4 to 6 servings

Full-flavored and hearty, this dish is ready for the table in 20 minutes or less. A full-bodied barbecue sauce, either bottled or the easy homemade version, gives it all the flavor it needs. Serve over hot cooked grains or with baked or microwaved sweet potatoes on the side. A simple slaw is the perfect foil for all barbecue-flavored dishes.

1½ tablespoons olive oil

1 medium onion, chopped

2 cloves garlic, minced, optional

1 (14-ounce) package vegan sausage, sliced ½ inch thick

2 (15-ounce) cans cannellini or navy beans, drained and rinsed or 3 cups cooked

1 cup barbecue sauce (your favorite variety) or Super-Quick No-Cook Barbecue Sauce (page 202)

4 to 5 ounces baby spinach

Hot cooked grains (rice, quinoa, couscous, or another grain), optional

1. Heat the oil in a wide skillet or stir-fry pan. Add the onions and sauté over medium heat until translucent, about 3 minutes.

2. Add the garlic, if using, and the vegan sausage, and continue to sauté, stirring frequently, until everything is golden, about 5 minutes.

3. Stir in the beans and barbecue sauce, and cook until piping hot, about 4 minutes.

4. Add the spinach and cover. When it wilts down a bit, which should take no longer than a minute, stir it into the mixture. Continue to cook for just a minute or so longer. Serve at once on its own or over hot cooked grains, if desired.

Vegan on a Budget

Mujaddara
(Middle Eastern Lentils & Rice)

6 servings

Mujaddara, a traditional Middle Eastern dish, is sometimes made with rice or, in certain regional variations, with cracked wheat or bulgur. Either way, the grain is combined with lentils and lots of onions, browned in olive oil. I like making this simple dish with brown rice, since it can be cooked together with the lentils. It's an appetizing dish—even if, admittedly, it isn't the prettiest.

Serve *Mujaddara* with a simple salad of finely chopped tomatoes, cucumbers, and peppers, dressed in olive oil and lemon juice. Or, for an easy addition that follows the Middle Eastern theme, I highly recommend Fattouche (page 149). If you are serving a bigger crowd, you can also add Homemade Hummus (page 200) and some fresh pita.

1 cup raw long- or medium-grain brown rice, rinsed

1 cup raw brown lentils, rinsed

1 vegetable bouillon cube

2 tablespoons olive oil

2 large onions, quartered and thinly sliced

½ cup finely chopped fresh parsley

2 scallions, thinly sliced (optional)

1 teaspoon ground cumin, or more, to taste

Salt and freshly ground pepper, to taste

1. Combine the rice, lentils, and bouillon cube with 5 cups of water in a medium saucepan. Bring to a slow boil, then lower the heat, cover, and simmer for 30 minutes, or until the water is absorbed. If either the rice or the lentils aren't done, add ½ cup of water and cook until all the water is absorbed. Repeat as needed.

2. Meanwhile, heat the oil in a wide skillet or stir-fry pan. Add the onions and cook over medium-low heat, stirring frequently, until lightly browned, about 15 minutes.

3. Add the rice and lentil mixture to the pan with the browned onions (if you'd like, set aside some of the onions for topping), and stir to combine. Stir in the remaining ingredients and cook over medium heat for a few minutes, then serve.

Black Bean Sofrito

4 to 6 servings

Inspired by a classic Puerto Rican dish, *sofrito* consists of a mixture of onions, garlic, bell peppers, tomatoes, and chili peppers. Taken together, they're a perfect flavoring blend for black beans. Fast and flavorful, this *sofrito* is served over rice, or as a great foundation for embellished rice bowls (see Variation).

1 tablespoon olive oil

1 large onion, finely chopped

3 to 4 cloves garlic, minced

1 medium green bell pepper, finely diced

1 cup finely diced ripe tomatoes

1 to 2 small hot chili peppers, seeded and minced, or dried hot red pepper flakes, to taste

2 (15-ounce) cans black beans, drained and rinsed, or 3 cups cooked black beans

2 teaspoons ground cumin

Juice of ½ to 1 lemon or lime, to taste

Salt and freshly ground pepper, to taste

Hot cooked rice (about 1 cup per serving)

Chopped parsley or cilantro, optional

1. Heat the oil in a large skillet. Add the onions and sauté over medium heat until translucent, about 3 minutes. Add the garlic and the bell pepper, and continue to sauté until all are golden, about 5 minutes longer.

2. Add the tomatoes, chili peppers, beans, cumin, and lemon juice. Stir in about ½ cup of water and bring the mixture to a simmer.

3. Mash enough of the black beans with the back of a large fork to thicken the base a bit. Continue to simmer gently over low heat, covered, for 5 to 7 minutes.

4. Season with salt and pepper, and serve over hot cooked rice, garnished with the parsley or cilantro, if desired.

VARIATION

To turn this into an appealing rice bowl, use shallow bowls for serving. Place a cup or so of hot cooked rice in each bowl, followed by a generous dollop of the black bean *sofrito*, arranged on one side. Choose two or three of the following, and arrange them nicely over the other side of the rice:

- Sautéed rounds of yellow squash
- Diced, roasted sweet potato or winter squash
- Lightly sautéed, slightly underripe banana
- Sliced avocado

Coconut Yellow Rice & Black Beans

6 to 8 servings

This versatile, sunshine-hued rice dish can be enjoyed on its own with a simple vegetable side dish or salad. And since it makes a generous helping, leftovers can be transformed into enticing bowls or used as a filling for burritos (see Variations).

1 tablespoon olive oil

1 large onion, finely chopped

2 to 3 cloves garlic, minced

1½ cups rice (use your favorite variety, white or brown)

1 (15-ounce) can light coconut milk

½ teaspoon turmeric

2 teaspoons salt-free seasoning (for more information, see page xxiii)

1 (15-ounce) can black beans, drained and rinsed

1 (16-ounce) bag frozen cauliflower, thawed

Juice of ½ lime (2 tablespoons), or more, to taste

Salt and freshly ground pepper, to taste
¼ cup chopped fresh parsley or cilantro, or as needed, optional

1. Heat the oil in a large skillet or stir-fry pan. Add the onions and sauté until translucent. Add the garlic and continue to sauté until both are golden.

2. Add the rice to the pan, along with the coconut milk and 2 cups of water. Bring to a slow boil, then stir in the turmeric and the salt-free seasoning blend. Lower the heat, cover, and simmer until the water is absorbed, about 15 minutes for white rice and 30 minutes for brown. If the rice isn't done to your liking, stir in an additional ½ cup of water, and continue to cook until the additional water is absorbed.

3. Stir in the black beans. Chop the cauliflower pieces up a bit if they're large, then stir them into the rice mixture. Cook for 6 to 8 minutes, or until everything is well heated through.

4. Season to taste with lime juice, salt, and pepper; stir in some parsley or cilantro, if desired, or sprinkle on individual servings as a garnish.

VARIATIONS

- BOWLS: Serve in shallow bowls, embellished with any of the ingredients suggested for *sofrito* bowls (page 40).

- BURRITOS OR WRAPS: Use this dish to make burritos or wraps (you can use reheated leftovers). Using burrito-sized tortillas or large wraps, place a generous dollop (about a cup, or what the tortilla will accommodate comfortably) in the center. Embellish with baby spinach or other tender greens and salsa. Tuck two sides of the tortilla over the filling, then roll up snugly.

Jamaican-Inspired
Rice & Red Beans

4 to 6 servings

This is a shortcut version of a traditional Jamaican favorite, simply called "rice and peas" (though the "peas" are actually small red beans) in the island nation. I first learned to make this the authentic way from a Jamaican friend. We cooked the beans from scratch and cracked open and grated a whole coconut. While it was a fun project, busy cooks can enjoy a quicker route to a satisfying dish.

My workarounds include canned coconut milk and canned beans (though you can certainly cook your own). If you have rice cooked ahead of time, even better! This goes especially well with Stir-Fried Collard Greens with Cabbage & Carrots (page 45). Or keep it simple with a steamed green vegetable—green beans, asparagus, or broccoli.

---

1 tablespoon olive oil

1 large onion, finely chopped

3 cloves garlic, minced

3½ to 4 cups cooked rice (any variety)

2 (15-ounce) cans small red beans, drained and rinsed, or 3 cups cooked

1 (15-ounce) can light coconut milk

1 teaspoon curry powder

1 to 2 small hot chili peppers, seeded and minced, optional

2 scallions, thinly sliced

¼ cup chopped fresh parsley or cilantro, optional

Salt and freshly ground pepper, to taste

1. Heat the oil in a small soup pot or stir-fry pan. Add the onions and sauté over medium-low heat until translucent. Add the garlic and continue to sauté until the onions are golden, about 5 minutes.

2. Add the rice, beans, coconut milk, curry powder, and chili peppers, if using. Bring to a simmer, then cover and cook over low heat for 10 to 15 minutes, or until most of the coconut milk is absorbed. The mixture should be moist, but not soupy.

3. Stir in the scallions and the parsley or cilantro, if using. Season with salt and pepper and serve.

Vegan on a Budget

Stir-Fried Collard Greens with Cabbage & Carrots

4 to 6 servings

Collard greens, with their impressively large leaves, might not be your first choice of vegetable to prep on a busy weeknight, but it's easier than it may seem, and they deserve a place in your rotation. To my taste buds, collards are more flavorful than kale. They're a touch sweeter, with no hint of bitterness, and they're an excellent source of calcium for the vegan diet. While many traditional recipes call for them to be cooked to death, they are quickly stir-fried here. The result is so much more appealing, for both the palate and the eyes!

1 (10- to 12-ounce) bunch collard greens

1½ tablespoons olive oil

2 to 3 cloves garlic, minced

1 cup pre-grated carrots or thin baby carrots

2 cups thinly sliced green or napa cabbage

2 scallions, thinly sliced

1 tablespoon lemon juice

Salt and freshly ground pepper, to taste

Pinch of dried hot red pepper flakes, optional

1. Cut the collard green leaves away from their stems with a sharp knife or kitchen shears. Stack 6 to 8 similar-sized leaf halves on top of one another. Roll them up snugly from one of the narrow ends, then slice thinly crosswise to form ribbons. Chop in a few places to shorten the ribbons. Repeat as needed. Place in a colander and rinse well.

2. Heat about half the oil in a wide skillet or stir-fry pan. Add the garlic and sauté for a minute or so over low heat.

3. Add the collard greens, then layer the carrots, cabbage, and scallions over them in that order. Turn the heat up to medium and add about ¼ cup of water. Cover and steam for about 3 to 4 minutes.

4. Drain off the water and drizzle in the remaining oil. Turn the heat up to medium-high and stir-fry the vegetables for 3 to 4 minutes longer, or until tender-crisp to your liking.

5. Drizzle in the lemon juice, season with salt and pepper, and add the red pepper flakes, if desired, for some heat. Serve at once.

Quinoa & Cauliflower Pilaf

4 to 6 servings

This simple skillet dish features two companionable ingredients—cauliflower and quinoa. Being on a budget doesn't mean you need to swear off a slightly more expensive grain like quinoa, since it's such a good value, nutrition-wise. It's nice to have an alternative to rice, and with quinoa, sometimes less goes a long way.

1 cup quinoa, any color, rinsed

2 vegetable bouillon cubes

1 tablespoon olive oil

1 medium yellow or red onion, finely chopped

1 (16-ounce) bag frozen cauliflower florets, thawed (see Note)

⅓ cup raisins or dried cranberries

¼ cup minced fresh parsley, or more, to taste

1 to 2 tablespoons lemon juice, to taste

Salt and freshly ground pepper, to taste

⅓ cup chopped toasted walnuts or ¼ cup toasted sunflower seeds

1. Combine the quinoa with the bouillon cubes and 2 cups of water in a saucepan. Bring to a slow boil, then cover and simmer gently for 15 minutes, or until all the water is absorbed.

2. Meanwhile, heat the oil in a wide skillet or stir-fry pan. Add the onions and sauté over medium-low heat until golden, about 5 minutes.

3. Add the cauliflower and about ¼ cup of water. Cover and cook for 3 to 4 minutes, or until the cauliflower is just tender.

4. Once the quinoa is done, add it to the cauliflower mixture, followed by the cranberries, parsley, and lemon juice. Toss together, then remove from the heat.

5. Season with salt and pepper. Scatter the nuts on top and serve at once.

NOTE

Frozen cauliflower is used here for weeknight convenience. Of course, if you prefer fresh or have extra time, by all means, swap it out for the frozen; 4 to 5 cups of bite-sized pieces should do the trick, and you'll need just a few extra minutes of cooking in step 3.

Gingery Red Beans & Broccoli with Bulgur or Quinoa

4 to 6 servings

Giving bean dishes an Asian spin might seem offbeat but the balance of colors, textures, and flavors in this dish works very well indeed. Inspired by dishes incorporating adzuki beans (small red beans used in Japanese cuisine), this is an excellent everyday dish that delivers your protein and vegetables in an appealing way. Any of the Simple Slaws on page 137 go well with it.

1½ tablespoons olive oil

1 large onion, quartered and thinly sliced

2 cloves garlic, minced

4 cups bite-sized broccoli florets

2 large ripe tomatoes, diced

2 (15-ounce) cans small red beans, drained and rinsed, or 3 cups cooked

1 tablespoon grated fresh or squeeze-bottle ginger, or to taste

¼ cup teriyaki marinade, bottled or homemade (page 199)

Hot cooked grain (rice, couscous, bulgur, or quinoa)

1. Heat the oil in a large skillet. Add the onions and sauté over medium heat until golden, about 5 minutes

2. Add the garlic and broccoli with enough water to keep the pan moist. Cover and steam until the broccoli is bright green, 2 to 3 minutes.

3. Add the tomatoes, beans, ginger, and teriyaki marinade. Bring to a simmer, then cook over low heat for 5 minutes longer, stirring occasionally.

4. Serve at once, on top of or alongside your hot cooked grain of choice.

Barbecue-Flavored Tofu & Chickpea Bowl

3 to 4 servings

Recently, I've noticed that bowl recipes in cookbooks and around the web have become quite complicated. A concept that started out as a simple way to enjoy variety in a meal has gone kind of crazy—sometimes 3 to 4 sauces have to be made with a plethora of spices, plus a myriad of ingredients have to be prepped just so. This gorgeous barbecue-flavored tofu and chickpea bowl dials the concept back quite a bit, yet is just as satisfying as any fancier bowl. And because it uses so few ingredients, you guessed it—it's more economical as well.

Base of your choice: Grains, noodles, or spiralized zucchini (see Note)

1 (8-ounce) package baked tofu (any variety)

1 (15- to 16-ounce) can chickpeas, drained and rinsed

¾ cup barbecue sauce (your favorite variety) or Super-Quick No-Cook Barbecue Sauce (page 202), or as needed

1 large broccoli crown, cut into bite-sized pieces

Olive oil, optional

1 medium avocado, peeled and sliced

1 heaping cup diced tomatoes or halved cherry or grape tomatoes

1 scallion, thinly sliced

1. Prepare the base of the bowl: Cook the grain or noodles according to package directions, if using. Set aside.

2. Meanwhile, cut the tofu into ½-inch dice. Combine the tofu, chickpeas, and about ¾ cup of barbecue sauce in a medium skillet, and bring it to a simmer. Cook for about 10 minutes, or until the chickpeas and tofu start to turn golden brown in spots. Remove from the heat and set aside.

3. Steam the broccoli briefly, just until bright green and tender-crisp. Drizzle with a little olive oil, if desired.

4. Assemble the bowls: For each serving, put some of your chosen base (grains, noodles, or spiralized zucchini) in the bottom of the bowl (no special amount, just use what you'd like).

5. Arrange some of the barbecue tofu and chickpeas in the center, then surround with some of the steamed broccoli, avocado, and cherry or grape tomatoes (cut in half if large; keep whole if desired).

6. Garnish with scallions and serve. Pass around extra barbecue sauce, if desired.

NOTE

You can use any kind of cooked grain, noodles, or zucchini noodles for the base of the bowl. For the grain, you can use quinoa, couscous, parboiled farro, or whatever you have on hand.

Tofu, Bok Choy
& Baby Corn Teriyaki

4 servings

Not only is this stir-fry quite colorful, there's very little chopping involved. The main feature is bok choy, one of my favorite vegetables, and one that gives you a lot of bang for the buck, especially in season. In most areas, that would be late spring and early fall. Though you wouldn't know to look at it, bok choy is a great source of calcium for the plant-based diet.

1 large or 2 smaller baby bok choy, or 4 to 5 stalks regular bok choy

1 (14-ounce) tub extra-firm tofu

1 to 2 tablespoons safflower or another neutral vegetable oil

1 cup baby carrots, quartered lengthwise if thick, or grated carrots

3 scallions, sliced

1 (15-ounce) can cut or whole baby corn, drained

¼ cup teriyaki marinade, bottled or homemade (page 199), plus more for serving

2 teaspoons grated fresh or squeeze-bottle ginger

OPTIONAL FOR SERVING

Hot cooked grains or noodles for serving

Peanuts or chopped cashews for topping

Sriracha or dried hot red pepper flakes

1. Prepare the bok choy: Remove and discard the stem ends, then slice the bok choy (leaves and ribs included) crosswise into strips. Rinse well in a colander to remove any grit. Set aside.

2. Cut the tofu into 8 slices crosswise and blot well between layers of paper toweling or a clean tea towel. Cut each slice in half to form squares, then cut each of the squares on the diagonal to form triangles. (Or you can just cut the tofu into small dice.)

3. Heat the oil in a stir-fry pan or a large skillet. When the oil is hot, add the tofu. Cook over high heat, stirring frequently, until the tofu is golden on most sides.

4. Add the carrots and stir-fry for another minute or two.

5. Add the bok choy, along with the scallions, baby corn, teriyaki marinade, and ginger, and stir-fry over high heat for just another minute or so. The bok choy should stay nice and crisp.

6. Serve at once on its own or over hot cooked grains or noodles. Top with some nuts and sprinkle with some sriracha or red pepper flakes to spice up the dish, if desired. Pass around extra teriyaki marinade as well.

Tofu & Broccoli
with Coconut Peanut Sauce

4 servings

In the mood for Thai? Using ready-made Thai peanut satay sauce, available in the Asian foods section of well-stocked supermarkets, gives this tofu dish lots of flavor with little effort. If you prefer, of course, you can go one step further and make your own Coconut Peanut Sauce or Dressing (page 203). Serve over rice or noodles, and add a Simple Slaw (page 137) or a platter of sliced bell peppers and tomatoes.

1 (14-ounce) tub extra-firm tofu

1 tablespoon safflower or another neutral vegetable oil

2 tablespoons soy sauce or tamari

2 large crowns broccoli, cut into bite-sized florets

1 cup (or more) white or brown mushrooms, cleaned, stemmed, and sliced

1 cup bottled Thai peanut satay sauce or Coconut Peanut Sauce or Dressing (page 203)

2 scallions, sliced

Dried hot red pepper flakes, to taste

Hot cooked rice or noodles for serving

Peanuts (crushed, if desired) for garnish, optional

1. Cut the tofu into ½-inch-thick slices and blot well between layers of paper toweling or a clean tea towel. Cut into ½-inch dice.

2. Heat the oil and soy sauce in a wide skillet or stir-fry pan, stirring them together. Add the tofu and stir quickly to coat. Cook over medium-high heat, stirring frequently, until golden brown and crisp on most sides, about 8 to 10 minutes.

3. Add the broccoli and mushrooms and cook, stirring frequently, just until the broccoli is bright green and tender-crisp. Add a little water to keep the pan moist.

4. Stir in the peanut sauce, scallions, and red pepper flakes. Serve at once over cooked rice or noodles. Pass around peanuts for topping individual servings, if desired.

Vegan on a Budget

Teriyaki
Fried Rice & Tofu

6 servings

If you're a rice and tofu fan, this stir-fry might earn a regular place in your culinary repertoire. Having the rice cooked ahead of time makes it especially quick to prepare. For a complete meal, all you need is a colorful salad, though serving vegetable spring rolls from the frozen foods section is a fun splurge.

Instead of dousing the dish with soy sauce, as I used to do, its flavor boost comes from using either teriyaki sauce or Korean barbecue marinade (a newer, and welcome addition to the Asian foods aisle in supermarkets). These kinds of bottled sauces have more complex flavor and add more than just saltiness to the dish. That said, you can make your own Teriyaki Marinade, if desired (page 199).

---

1 (14-ounce) tub extra-firm tofu

1 tablespoon safflower or another neutral vegetable oil

1 tablespoon soy sauce or tamari

1 medium red bell pepper, diced or cut into strips

2 cloves garlic, minced

4 to 5 cups cooked long-grain brown or white rice

⅓ cup teriyaki or Korean barbecue marinade, or more, to taste

4 scallions (white and green parts), thinly sliced

2 teaspoons grated fresh or squeeze-bottle ginger

Freshly ground pepper or dried hot red pepper flakes, to taste

½ cup peanut halves, or as desired

1. Cut the tofu into 6 slabs crosswise and blot well between layers of paper toweling or a clean tea towel. Cut the slabs into dice.

2. Heat the oil and soy sauce in a large skillet or stir-fry pan, stirring them together. Add the tofu and stir quickly to coat. Cook over medium-high heat, stirring frequently, until golden brown on most sides. This can take up to 10 minutes.

3. Stir in the bell peppers and garlic, and cook over medium-high heat for 2 minutes.

4. Add the cooked rice, marinade, scallions, and ginger. Stir together and continue to cook until the rice is piping hot, about 5 minutes, stirring often.

5. Season with pepper and more marinade, if desired. Serve at once. Pass around peanuts for topping individual servings.

Seitan & Broccoli Stir-Fry

4 servings

Here's a simple stir-fry featuring the unique flavor and texture of high-protein seitan. The recipe calls for either teriyaki marinade or Korean barbecue sauce (which is available in the Asian foods section of any well-stocked supermarket). I've come to consider Korean barbecue marinade a staple; I love that it has a slightly sweet and spicy kick to it. If you prefer, you can make your own Teriyaki Marinade (page 199). And, if you like seitan, I highly recommend learning to make your own (page 192). It's easy once you get the hang of it, and quite a money-saver when a recipe calls for a generous quantity.

1 tablespoon safflower or another neutral vegetable oil

1 tablespoon soy sauce

1 pound seitan, packaged or homemade (page 192), cut into bite-sized chunks

2 medium broccoli crowns, cut into bite-sized pieces

1 medium red bell pepper, diced

2 to 3 scallions, sliced

¼ cup teriyaki marinade (bottled or homemade, page 199) or Korean barbecue marinade, plus more for serving

2 teaspoons grated fresh or squeeze-bottle ginger

Hot cooked rice or noodles

Sriracha or another hot sauce, optional

1. Heat the oil and soy sauce in a stir-fry pan or large skillet. Add the seitan and stir-fry for 5 to 6 minutes, or until touched with golden-brown spots here and there. Transfer to a bowl and set aside.

2. Add the broccoli, bell peppers, and scallions to the same pan, with a little water to keep the vegetables moist. Stir-fry for 3 to 4 minutes, or until the vegetables are just tender-crisp.

3. Return the seitan to the pan, along with the teriyaki or Korean barbecue marinade and ginger. Stir together with the vegetables, then stir-fry for just a minute or so longer.

4. Serve at once over cooked rice or noodles. Pass around additional teriyaki or Korean barbecue marinade for seasoning individual portions, as well as the sriracha, if desired.

3

COZY CASSEROLES & OTHER BAKED DISHES

You don't have to travel back to the 1950s to enjoy cozy casseroles and similar baked dishes. A generous pan of this kind of comforting fare goes a long way, both in terms of the pocketbook and keeping the happy eater full and satisfied. Tortilla casseroles, potato and rice casseroles, baked pasta dishes, and more make heaping helpings and are among the kinds of recipes that are bound to become family favorites. Several of the recipes in this chapter are excellent choices for potlucks or served as holiday fare.

Enchilada Casserole

8 servings

Filled with Southwestern flavors, and yielding a generous amount, this is a good candidate to become your go-to casserole. It calls for both beans and vegan beefy crumbles, but if you'd like, you can omit the crumbles and double up on the beans; it's excellent either way. Complete the meal with a green salad, and while you have the oven on, consider making a pan of Roasted Root Vegetables with Brussels Sprouts (page 72).

1 (15- to 16-ounce) can tomato sauce or crushed tomatoes

1 tablespoon olive oil

1 (15-ounce) can pinto, pink, or black beans, drained and rinsed

1 (10-ounce) bag vegan beefy crumbles (or omit and use another can of beans)

1 (1½-ounce) packet taco seasoning

1 cup salsa, plus more for topping

2 cups frozen corn kernels, thawed

2 to 3 scallions, thinly sliced (reserve some for topping)

10 to 12 corn tortillas

1½ to 2 cups cups vegan cheddar or pepper jack cheese shreds

1. Preheat the oven to 400°F and lightly oil a wide 2-quart casserole dish.

2. Pour about ¼ cup of the tomato sauce on the bottom of the prepared casserole dish and spread it around evenly.

3. Heat the oil in a large skillet or stir-fry pan. Add the beans and beefy crumbles (or the extra can of beans, if you prefer), the remaining tomato sauce, and the taco seasoning.

4. Stir together and bring to a simmer over medium-high heat for 5 minutes.

5. Stir in the salsa, corn, and scallions and cook for 2 minutes longer. Remove from the heat.

6. Layer in the casserole dish as follows: 5 to 6 tortillas (enough to cover; sometimes it's easier to cover the surface evenly if you cut them in half), overlapping one another; half of the bean mixture; half of the cheese. Repeat the layers. Sprinkle some scallions on top.

7. Bake for 15 to 20 minutes, until the cheese is nicely melted and the casserole is well heated through. Let stand for a minute or 2, then cut into squares to serve. Pass around salsa to top each serving.

Taco Casserole

6 to 8 servings

This recipe makes Taco Tuesday even easier by converting individual tacos into a flavorful and fun casserole. Corn tortillas form the bottom layer, followed by a bean layer and vegan cheese. Once out of the oven, the final layer is the cool stuff—lettuce, tomato, and avocado. If you like tacos, but not the tendency for the tasty stuff to fall out of the tortillas, this casserole solves that problem neatly, or at least more neatly. Watch this hot and cool casserole disappear quickly.

2 (15-ounce) cans black or pinto beans (or one of each), drained and rinsed

1 cup salsa (your favorite variety)

1 tablespoon barbecue seasoning (for more information, see page xxii), or 1 (1½-ounce) packet taco seasoning

8 to 10 corn tortillas

1½ cups vegan cheddar or pepper jack cheese shreds

½ head romaine lettuce, cut into shreds

2 medium tomatoes, diced

OPTIONAL TOPPINGS

Tofu Sour Cream (page 198)

1 ripe avocado, peeled, mashed, and tossed with lemon or lime juice

Extra salsa (your favorite variety)

Hot sauce of your choice

1. Preheat the oven to 400°F and lightly oil a large rectangular casserole dish (about 9 × 13 inches).

2. Combine the beans, salsa, and seasoning in a bowl and stir together.

3. Line the bottom of the prepared casserole dish with the corn tortillas, overlapping as needed. Spread the bean layer evenly over the tortillas, followed by the cheese.

4. Bake for 15 to 20 minutes, or until the cheese is melted and the casserole is heated through.

5. Let the casserole stand for a minute or two, then cut into squares. Top the casserole with the lettuce and tomatoes. Serve at once. Pass around any or all of the optional toppings.

Vegan Carne Asada Fries

4 to 6 servings

A unique combination of French fries, avocado, sour cream, and, in its original form, strip steak, this dish originated in San Diego in the 1990s and soon became a standard in casual Mexican restaurants in the American Southwest. Now it's on menus nationwide. This plant-based version replaces the meat with seitan. It might still seem a bit odd, but it's so tasty that it's easy to see why it spread like wildfire.

FOR THE BAKED FRIES (OR SEE NOTE)

2 pounds medium potatoes, preferably golden, scrubbed well

1 tablespoon olive oil
Salt and pepper, to taste

FOR THE SEITAN "CARNE"

½ cup salsa (your favorite variety)

1 tablespoon olive oil

2 teaspoons barbecue seasoning (for more information, see page xxii)

16 ounces seitan, homemade (page 192) or packaged, drained and cut into strips

FOR THE AVOCADO AND TOMATO TOPPING

1 medium or 2 small ripe avocados, peeled and diced

1 cup diced tomato or halved cherry tomatoes

Juice of ½ lime

Handful of chopped fresh cilantro

2 scallions, green parts only, thinly sliced

OPTIONAL GARNISHES

Tofu Sour Cream (page 198)

Lime wedges

1. Preheat the oven to 425°F and line one baking sheet and one roasting pan with parchment paper.

2. Prepare the baked fries: Cut the potatoes in half lengthwise, then cut each half into 4 wedges and place them in a mixing bowl. Drizzle in the olive oil and sprinkle with salt and pepper, then stir to coat. Transfer to the lined baking sheet, reserving the bowl for preparing the seitan "carne."

3. Prepare the seitan "carne": Stir together the salsa, olive oil, and barbecue seasoning in the same bowl used to prepare the fries. Add the seitan and stir to coat. Transfer to the lined roasting pan.

4. Place the fries and the seitan mixture in the oven and bake for 25 minutes, stirring both of them a couple of times during baking, until the fries are golden brown and crisp, and the seitan is sizzling hot.

5. Meanwhile, prepare the avocado and tomato topping: Combine all the topping ingredients in a small bowl and toss gently.

6. To serve, distribute the fries among the individual plates. Top with some seitan strips, then the avocado and tomato topping. Add a dollop of the sour cream and/or a lime wedge or two, if desired. Serve at once.

Skinny Scalloped Potatoes

4 to 6 servings

Here's a deceptively rich-tasting version of scalloped potatoes, a recipe that in its original form uses a number of high-fat dairy products. This one is made with a creamy sauce of silken tofu or white beans, adding both heft and protein.

6 large or 8 medium potatoes, preferably red-skinned or golden

2 cups finely chopped fresh or frozen (thawed) broccoli or cauliflower

2 tablespoons olive oil or vegan butter

1 large or 2 medium onions, quartered and thinly sliced

1 (12.3-ounce) package firm silken tofu or 1 (15-ounce) can white beans, drained and rinsed

½ cup unsweetened nondairy milk

Salt and freshly ground pepper, to taste

1 cup breadcrumbs

Finely chopped fresh parsley, optional

1. Scrub the potatoes and microwave them until they're done but still firm. Start with a minute per potato and test; increase time as needed. When they're cool enough to handle (plunge them into cold water to speed up the process), cut them into ¼-inch-thick slices.

2. If you're using fresh broccoli or cauliflower, steam in a small saucepan or skillet with a little water until tender, but not overdone. If you're using frozen, just make sure it's completely thawed.

3. Preheat the oven to 375°F and lightly oil a 1½-quart shallow baking dish.

4. Heat the 2 tablespoons of oil in a medium skillet. Add the onions and sauté over medium heat until they're soft and golden, about 5 to 7 minutes.

5. Combine the tofu or beans, half of the onions (set the rest aside), and the nondairy milk in a food processor or blender, and blend until completely pureed.

6. Transfer the puree to a large mixing bowl, along with the potato slices and the cauliflower. Stir together; don't worry if the potato slices break apart.

7. Season with salt and pepper. If it seems like there's too much sauce for the potatoes, don't worry—a lot of it gets absorbed while baking. Transfer the mixture to the prepared baking dish and pat it down evenly. Top with the reserved onions, followed by the breadcrumbs.

8. Bake until the top is golden and slightly crusty, about 30 to 40 minutes. Top with the parsley, if using, and let cool for 5 minutes, then cut into squares to serve.

VARIATION

▪ Substitute a sweet potato or two for some of the regular potatoes.

Vegan Poutine
(Cheese & Gravy-Smothered Fries)

4 or more servings

Poutine is a Canadian fast-food specialty with roots in Quebec. Like Carne Asada Fries (page 62), it grew from a local specialty, this one in Montreal, to achieve nationwide popularity. Basically, it consists of French fries smothered in gravy and topped with cheese, and, yes, it's a bit odd, but somehow it really works. This vegan poutine recipe swaps out beefy gravy for mushroom gravy, and, of course, uses nondairy cheese.

I like to serve something fresh and green with this dish—ideally, a colorful green salad and/or a big batch of broccoli or other vegetables that can be roasted while the poutine is in the oven.

FOR THE BAKED FRIES (OR SEE NOTE)

- 2 pounds medium potatoes, preferably golden, scrubbed well
- 1 tablespoon olive oil
- Salt and freshly ground pepper, to taste

FOR THE MUSHROOM GRAVY

- 1 large or 2 regular vegetable bouillon cubes
- 6 to 8 ounces cremini (baby bella) or white mushrooms, cleaned, stemmed, and sliced
- 2 tablespoons soy sauce or tamari
- 2½ tablespoons cornstarch or arrowroot
- Pinch of Italian seasoning, optional
- 2 tablespoons nutritional yeast, optional (but highly recommended)

FOR THE TOPPINGS

- 1 to 1½ cups vegan cheddar cheese shreds, as desired
- 2 to 3 scallions, thinly sliced

1. Preheat the oven to 425°F and line a baking sheet or roasting pan with parchment paper.

2. Prepare and bake the fries: Cut the potatoes in half lengthwise, then cut each half into 4 wedges and place in a mixing bowl. Drizzle in the olive oil and sprinkle with salt and pepper, then stir to coat. Transfer to the lined baking sheet or roasting pan. Bake the potatoes, stirring occasionally, for 25 minutes, or until golden and crisp. Remove from the oven, but keep the oven on.

3. When the fries are nearly done, make the mushroom gravy: Combine 1¼ cups of water, bouillon cubes, mushrooms, and soy sauce in a small saucepan and bring to a slow boil. Turn down the heat and simmer until the mushrooms are wilted, about 5 minutes.

4. Meanwhile, combine the cornstarch with just enough water to make it smooth and pourable.

5. Slowly whisk the dissolved cornstarch into the simmering broth, stirring constantly with a whisk, until the mixture is thickened.

6. Remove from the heat and whisk in the Italian seasoning and the nutritional yeast, if using. Transfer about half of the gravy to a spouted container and reserve the rest in the pan.

7. Assemble and bake the casserole: When the fries are done, transfer them to a lightly oiled shallow 1½-quart casserole dish. Pour the gravy remaining in the saucepan over them, followed by an even sprinkling of the vegan cheese and the scallions. Bake for 5 to 8 minutes longer, or until the cheese is melted.

8. Serve at once, passing around the gravy in the spouted container.

NOTE

Cutting 2 pounds of potatoes into fry shapes isn't a whole lot of work, but if you'd like to skip this step you can use two 16-ounce bags of all-natural frozen fries.

VARIATION

- To make this more of a protein dish, add an 8-ounce package of baked tofu (cut into strips) or an 8- to 10-ounce package of your favorite plant-based meat alternative. Vegan chick'n strips, beefy tips, or sausage all work.

Easy Oven Fries

Baked oven fries are a familiar, inexpensive side dish. When you're in the mood for them, make whatever quantity you need, according to how many people you're serving. Allow for one large or two medium potatoes or sweet potatoes per person. For regular potatoes, use golden or red-skinned varieties. One large sweet potato can stretch to two servings. If you're using organic potatoes, you can scrub them well and leave the skins on. Otherwise, peel and cut them into long, fry-shaped strips, about ½ inch thick.

Smaller potatoes can be cut into wedges—first quarter them, then cut each quarter in half.

In a mixing bowl, combine the cut potatoes with a drizzle of olive oil and toss well to coat. Transfer to a parchment-lined baking pan or roasting pan. Bake in a preheated 425°F oven, stirring every 10 minutes, until the potatoes are crisp and lightly browned, about 20 to 30 minutes. Season with salt and pepper and/or your favorite seasoning blend, such as Italian or salt-free seasoning.

Loaded Sweet Potatoes

2 servings

For this recipe, I'm offering up a smaller yield than usual (just two servings), because it's a perfect recipe for one (with leftovers) or two. On the other hand, it can be easily doubled or tripled to serve more. In fact, when you make these sweet potatoes, loaded up with familiar Southwestern flavors, there's no need for exact measuring. The quantity of each embellishment also depends on the size of the sweet potatoes. Almost a meal in itself, you can accompany these beauties with salsa and chips. Add a Simple Slaw (page 137) or salad, if you'd like.

2 large sweet potatoes

1 cup cooked or canned (drained and rinsed) black beans

½ cup lightly cooked fresh or frozen (thawed) corn kernels

½ cup salsa (your favorite variety)

½ cup vegan cheddar or pepper jack cheese shreds, or as desired

½ medium ripe avocado, peeled and cut into small dice

¼ cup chopped fresh cilantro

1 lime, cut into quarters

Hot seasoning or sauce (such as picante sauce or sriracha), optional

1. Preheat the oven to 375°F.

2. Microwave the sweet potatoes until soft but not mushy. Allow 3 minutes per sweet potato; test to see if it can be easily pierced, then add another minute or two as needed.

3. When the sweet potatoes can be handled (plunge them into cold water to speed up the process), split them in half lengthwise and mash the flesh with a fork. Arrange in a baking dish or a roasting pan. Smash them a bit more, using a spatula.

4. Combine the beans, corn, and salsa in a small bowl, and stir together. Distribute over the surface of the sweet potatoes, followed by the cheese.

5. Bake for 10 to 15 minutes, or until everything is piping hot and the cheese is melted.

6. Arrange two sweet potato halves on each plate, then top with avocado and cilantro. Serve with lime quarters for squeezing and pass around hot seasoning, if desired.

Lasagna-Like Pasta Casserole

8 or more servings

Lasagna is always such a hit, whether you make it for your family or to share at larger gatherings. But I find it a bit of a pain to make, what with having to arrange the noodles just so. And if you want to save time and effort by using no-cook noodles, you've got to be aware that it's hard to find a vegan brand (they often contain egg).

Here's an easy vegan baked pasta casserole that has all the great flavors of lasagna without the hassle. Plus, it only needs about 20 to 25 minutes in the oven—just enough time for the cheese to melt and the flavors to meld. It almost goes without saying that you can vary the vegetables; suggestions follow the recipe. A colorful salad is all that's needed to complete the meal, but it never hurts to add a green vegetable, like asparagus, green beans, or broccoli.

1 pound pasta (any short shape like shells, twists, or bowties)

1 (28-ounce) jar good-quality marinara sauce

1 (15-ounce) can crushed tomatoes

2 teaspoons Italian seasoning

8 ounces white or cremini (baby bella) mushrooms, cleaned, stemmed, and thinly sliced

1 medium zucchini, thinly sliced

1 (12.3-ounce) package firm or extra-firm silken tofu, well mashed

8 ounces vegan mozzarella cheese shreds

1. Preheat the oven to 400°F and lightly oil a 2-quart casserole dish (if you don't have one this large, split this recipe between 2 casserole dishes).

2. Cook the pasta according to the package directions until al dente, then drain and return it to the pot. Pour in the marinara, crushed tomatoes, and Italian seasoning. Stir to combine with the pasta.

3. Pour half of the pasta into the prepared casserole dish, then arrange the sliced mushrooms and zucchini over it. Layer the mashed tofu over the vegetables. Follow with a layer of half of the mozzarella shreds.

4. Finally, pour in the remaining pasta mixture and sprinkle with the remaining mozzarella shreds.

5. Cover the casserole with foil and bake for 15 minutes, then uncover and bake for 10 minutes longer. Remove from the oven, let it stand for 5 minutes or so, then serve.

NOTE

You can assemble the casserole in the morning or a day ahead of time and refrigerate it, covered. About a half hour before you'd like to serve it, bake at 400°F as directed.

VARIATIONS

- Substitute other vegetables for the ones recommended here. Small broccoli or cauliflower florets, chopped chard or kale, and diced eggplant are all great choices. You'll want to use 4 to 5 cups of vegetables in all, and, in the case of these particular vegetables, lightly steam them. You can also add a layer of baby spinach to any of these combinations or the one given in the main recipe.

VARIATIONS

■ Choose 3 or 4 of the following vegetables: cauliflower, broccoli, carrots, zucchini, yellow summer squash, mushrooms, kale, green peas, and corn kernels. All should be finely chopped (except in the case of green peas and corn) and lightly steamed before adding in step 3.

Vegetable & Chickpea Potpie

Makes 2 pies, serving 12

Everyone loves the nostalgic classic vegetable potpie, whether for everyday meals or as a crowd-pleasing vegan option for holidays. Pie crusts are usually sold in pairs; that's one reason I chose to have this recipe make two pies. The other is that it always disappears quickly, and those with bigger appetites will want seconds. It also freezes well. However, if you only want to make one pie, it is easy to cut this recipe in half.

8 medium potatoes

2 tablespoons olive oil

1 large onion, quartered and finely chopped

3 cups diced vegetables of your choice (see Variations)

1 (15-ounce) can chickpeas, drained (reserve liquid) and rinsed

1½ tablespoons all-purpose seasoning

¼ cup minced fresh parsley

Salt and freshly ground pepper, to taste

2 (9-inch), prepared, good-quality pie crusts, preferably whole grain

1 cup fine breadcrumbs

Paprika, optional

1. Cook or microwave the potatoes in their skins until done. (If you're microwaving, start with a minute per potato and test; increase time as needed.) When they're cool enough to handle (plunge them into a bowl of cold water to speed up the process), peel them. Dice 4 of them and mash the other 4 coarsely. Set aside until needed.

2. Preheat the oven to 350°F.

3. Heat the oil in a large skillet. Add the onions and sauté over medium heat until they're golden. Add the vegetables of your choice as well as the chickpeas, plus ¼ cup of their liquid.

4. Stir in both the diced and the mashed potatoes. Heat through gently. Stir in the all-purpose seasoning and parsley. Season with salt and pepper.

5. Divide the mixture between the 2 pie crusts and pat down. Sprinkle the breadcrumbs evenly over each pie, then top with a sprinkling of paprika, if using.

6. Bake for 35 to 40 minutes, or until the crust is golden. Let the pies stand at room temperature for 10 minutes or so, then cut into wedges and serve.

Roasted Root Vegetables
with Brussels Sprouts

6 servings

Oven-roasting brings out the natural sweetness of many vegetables—especially root vegetables. Even seasonings are optional, because roasting yields such incredible flavors. In most cases, just the lightest sprinkling of salt and pepper is all you'll need. This medley goes one flavor notch higher with the subtle kick of vinegar and maple syrup.

The nice thing about almost any kind of roasted vegetable preparation is that you don't have to slavishly follow the recipe—there's not much more to it than cut, toss with oil, and roast in a hot oven until lightly and evenly golden. You can vary the vegetables suggested here, as well as the amounts (see Variations).

2 medium beets, peeled and cut into bite-sized chunks (see Note)

6 medium carrots, halved lengthwise and cut into 3-inch sections (or 2 cups baby carrots)

1 pound tiny new potatoes or fingerlings, washed and cut in half

½ pound Brussels sprouts, trimmed and halved

1 medium onion, quartered and sliced

1 tablespoon olive oil

2 tablespoons maple syrup

1 tablespoon vinegar (apple cider, red wine, or balsamic)

Salt and freshly ground pepper, to taste

Fresh rosemary or dill for garnish, optional

1. Preheat the oven to 425°F and line a roasting pan with parchment paper.

2. Prepare all the vegetables as directed, and place them in a large mixing bowl.

3. Combine the oil, syrup, and vinegar in a small bowl and whisk together. Drizzle over the vegetables and stir together.

4. Transfer the mixture to the lined roasting pan. Bake for 25 to 30 minutes, stirring every 10 minutes or so. The vegetables should be tender on the inside and touched with golden brown on the outside.

5. Season with salt and pepper, then transfer to a covered serving container and keep warm until serving. Garnish with the fresh rosemary or dill, if desired.

NOTE

Peeling raw beets is challenging. Partially cooking them, either in a saucepan covered in water or in the microwave (about 2 minutes per raw beet) really helps. Cook just until you can poke through about a quarter inch into the beet. Let the beets cool to room temperature (if you need to expedite this, plunge them into a bowl of ice water). To minimize the mess when cutting, peel the beets over the trash can or a compost container, then slice or chop them on a cutting board covered with wax paper.

VARIATIONS

- Stir in ribbons of collard greens or lacinato kale about 10 minutes before the vegetables are done.
- Other root vegetables that work well are sweet potatoes, parsnips, daikon radishes, turnips, and rutabagas.
- Try cauliflower and/or broccoli in place of Brussels sprouts.
- Add some chopped garlic to the mix for even deeper flavor.
- To make this a main dish, serve the vegetables on a bed of cooked lentils or quinoa.

Not-Just-for-Holidays Green Bean Casserole

6 to 8 servings

What would the holidays be without green bean casserole? Well, here it is in an updated, veganized, and healthier version. Frozen green beans are used here, because, let's face it, we're lucky to have a month or two in midsummer when they're really good. This is a prime example of how useful and convenient frozen vegetables can be.

2 tablespoons olive oil

2 large onions, halved and thinly sliced

1 cup cooked or canned cannellini beans, drained and rinsed, or about half of one 12.3-ounce container extra-firm silken tofu

2 tablespoons flour (see Note)

8 ounces white or brown mushrooms, cleaned, stemmed, and sliced

2 (16-ounce) bags frozen cut green beans, thawed completely

Salt and freshly ground pepper, to taste

1 cup fine fresh breadcrumbs

1. Heat the oil in a medium skillet. Add the onions and sauté over medium heat until golden and just starting to brown, stirring often, about 8 minutes.

2. Transfer half of the onions to a food processor, along with the cannellini beans or silken tofu. Process until completely smooth.

3. Preheat the oven to 375°F and lightly oil a 2-quart casserole dish (or 2 smaller casserole dishes).

4. Sprinkle the flour over the remaining onions in the pan and stir until evenly coated. Raise the heat to medium-high and cook, stirring often, until they're browned (but not burned), about 5 to 7 minutes. Remove the pan from the heat. Transfer the onions to a plate and set aside.

5. Wipe out the pan and add the mushrooms with a little water. Cover and cook over medium heat until wilted, about 5 to 7 minutes. Drain off excess liquid.

6. Combine the bean or tofu puree, mushrooms, and green beans in a large mixing bowl and stir together. Season with salt and pepper.

7. Transfer the mixture to the prepared casserole dish. Top with the reserved onions, followed by the breadcrumbs.

8. Bake for 30 minutes, or until the breadcrumbs are lightly browned and crisp. Let the casserole stand at room temperature for 5 to 10 minutes, then serve.

NOTE

Use garbanzo flour, unbleached white flour, whole wheat pastry flour, or any flour you have on hand.

Green Rice Casserole

6 or more servings

Reminiscent of those old-fashioned recipes found in spiral-bound community cookbooks, this kind of casserole is a reminder of why comfort food is timeless. Now, with meltable nondairy cheese, there's a way to make this classic vegan. With plenty of broccoli and parsley, this rice casserole is as wholesome as it is addictive. Since you have the oven on at 400°F, consider making Roasted Root Vegetables with Brussels Sprouts (page 72) at the same time, or just roast a favorite vegetable or two.

2 tablespoons olive oil or vegan butter

1 large or 2 medium onions, finely chopped

2 large celery stalks, finely diced

4 cups finely chopped broccoli florets (some stems are fine)

½ cup finely chopped fresh parsley

2 tablespoons finely chopped fresh dill, optional

3½ to 4 cups cooked brown rice

2 cups vegan cheddar cheese shreds

½ cup unsweetened nondairy milk (for more information, see page xix)

2 teaspoons Italian seasoning

Salt and freshly ground pepper, to taste

1 cup fresh breadcrumbs for topping, optional

1. Preheat the oven to 400°F and lightly oil a 1½-quart round or oblong casserole dish.

2. Heat the oil or vegan butter in a large skillet or stir-fry pan. Add the onions and sauté over medium heat until golden.

3. Add the celery and broccoli, along with just enough water to keep the pan moist. Cover and cook just until the broccoli is tender-crisp and bright green. Remove from the heat.

4. Stir in the remaining ingredients, except for the optional breadcrumbs. Transfer the mixture to the prepared casserole dish and pat down evenly. Top with the breadcrumbs, if using.

5. Bake for 35 to 40 minutes, or until the edges are a bit crusty and the top is golden. Allow the casserole to stand for 5 minutes or so, then serve. Either cut into neat segments or just spoon it out.

4

NOODLING AROUND
IN THE KITCHEN

One-pound boxes of pasta are one of the best food bargains around, making this staple a perfect base for inexpensive main dishes. The trick is to turn the comforting blank canvas of pasta into a delivery system for vegetables and plant proteins. We'll also be exploring low-cost, high-flavor ways to use budget-friendly Asian noodles. From familiar Italian classics to more exotic (but not expensive) recipes, you'll be using your noodle wisely. Make sure, also, to see the Lasagna-Like Pasta Casserole recipe (page 68) in the previous chapter.

Pasta Primavera

6 servings

Although this dish uses less than a full pound of pasta, the generous amount of vegetables yields a heaping helping. Zucchini and yellow summer squash are economical all year round, and in the spring, its true season, asparagus is a bargain as well. Using seasonal vegetables is always best, but feel free to vary the vegetables in this recipe, using whatever you have in the fridge (see Variations). Serve with a simple green salad with tomatoes and chickpeas for a satisfying meal.

Adding vegan meatballs, as you can see in the photo, makes this dish even heartier. They might count as a splurge ingredient, but not necessarily. I used Earth Grown Organic Vegan Meatballs from the local Aldi market, which offers plant-based meat alternatives at amazing prices. You can explore similar markets and even online sources for good deals.

---

10 to 12 ounces pasta (any short shape)

2 tablespoons olive oil, divided

1 medium onion, quartered and thinly sliced

3 to 4 cloves garlic, minced

12 to 15 stalks asparagus, bottoms trimmed, cut into 1-inch lengths

2 medium yellow summer squashes or zucchini, or 1 of each, halved lengthwise and sliced

1 (28-ounce) can tomatoes, preferably fire-roasted

1 cup frozen green peas, thawed

2 teaspoons Italian seasoning

¼ to ½ cup chopped fresh parsley

Salt and freshly ground pepper, to taste

Dried hot red pepper flakes, to taste (optional)

Easiest Vegan Parmesan (page 87) or vegan mozzarella cheese shreds, optional

1. Cook the pasta according to the package directions until al dente, then drain.

2. Meanwhile, heat 1 tablespoon of the oil in a large skillet or stir-fry pan. Add the onions and sauté over medium heat until translucent. Add the garlic and continue to sauté until the onions are golden.

3. Add the asparagus and squashes and continue to sauté until just barely tender-crisp. Stir in the tomatoes, peas, and Italian seasoning. and continue to cook until just heated through. (You want the vegetables to stay crisp and colorful.)

4. Combine the vegetable mixture with the pasta in the pasta pot or in a large serving bowl. Toss to combine. Stir in the remaining tablespoon of olive oil and parsley, and season with salt and pepper, plus the dried hot red pepper flakes, if using.

5. Serve at once, passing around the vegan Parmesan or vegan mozzarella shreds for topping individual servings, if desired.

VARIATIONS

■ Instead of summer squash, try eggplant or broccoli. Green beans can stand in for asparagus.

OPTIONAL ADDITION

■ Use a package of your favorite brand of vegan meatballs. Heat the meatballs according to the package directions while the pasta is warming up.

Pasta Puttanesca
(Pasta with Olive Sauce)

4 servings

This Neopolitan recipe, originally named in Italian for ladies of the night, is simple, yet luscious. Like many pasta dishes, the sauce doesn't take longer to make than the time it takes for the pasta to cook, if you choose olives that are already pitted from your supermarket's olive bar. Complete this meal with a colorful salad with added chickpeas or another type of bean.

1 pound pasta (any long shape, like spaghetti or linguine)

1 tablespoon olive oil

2 to 3 cloves garlic, minced

1 large green bell pepper, diced

1 (14-ounce) can fire-roasted or Italian-style diced tomatoes

1 (28-ounce) jar marinara sauce (your favorite variety)

1 cup chopped, pitted brine-cured olives (use a combination of black and green if you'd like)

¼ cup dry white wine or red wine, optional

¼ cup finely chopped fresh parsley

Freshly ground pepper, to taste

Easiest Vegan Parmesan (page 87), optional

1. Cook the pasta according to the package directions until al dente, then drain.

2. Heat the oil in a large saucepan. Add the garlic and bell pepper and sauté over low heat until golden.

3. Add the tomatoes, marinara sauce, olives, and optional wine. Turn the heat up to medium-high and bring to a slow boil, then remove from the heat.

4. Combine the pasta with the olive sauce in a large serving bowl. Add the parsley, season with pepper, and toss well. Serve at once, passing around the Easiest Vegan Parmesan for topping individual servings, if desired.

Gnocchi
with Greens & Beans

4 to 6 servings

Gnocchi, an Italian specialty made of potato flour combined with semolina flour (the usual flour used in pastas), is a bit of starchy comfort heaven. They're wonderful with greens and beans—a classic Italian trio.

While some cooks like to make their own gnocchi (surely the homemade variety is best if you know what you're doing), the project takes hours and makes a floury mess of the kitchen. I've decided to take a pass here and use the ready-made kind. There are a number of vegan brands, but do read the package ingredients because gnocchi sometimes contain eggs. You'll find them in the frozen foods or fresh pasta sections of supermarkets and specialty groceries.

1 (16-ounce) package frozen gnocchi

1 tablespoon olive oil

2 to 3 cloves garlic, finely chopped

1 (28-ounce) jar marinara sauce

1 (15-ounce) can pink or white beans (cannellini), drained and rinsed

1 (5- to 6-ounce) package baby spinach, rinsed

½ cup pitted brined-cured black olives, chopped, or sliced sun-dried tomatoes

Salt and freshly ground pepper, to taste

Easiest Vegan Parmesan (page 87), optional

1. Cook the gnocchi according to the package directions, then drain.

2. Meanwhile, heat the oil in a large skillet or stir-fry pan. Add the garlic and sauté over low heat for a minute or two, until golden.

3. Add the marinara sauce and beans. Bring to a slow simmer, then add the spinach, in batches if necessary. Cover and cook just until wilted down.

4. Add the olives and cooked gnocchi, and stir everything together.

5. Season with salt (you may not need much salt, if any, so taste first) and pepper. Serve at once, passing around the Easiest Vegan Parmesan for topping individual servings, if desired.

Vegan on a Budget

Pasta Curry
with Spinach & Lentils

6 servings

Spinach and lentils are a classic pairing in Indian dishes. Combining them with a pasta curry is a bit of a stretch, but it does work! For a quick weeknight meal, I like to serve this with fresh flatbread and cucumbers, dressed in a creamy vegan dressing.

1 pound pasta (any short shape)

1½ tablespoons olive oil

1 medium onion, finely chopped

2 cloves garlic, minced

1 red bell pepper, diced

1 (14-ounce) can diced tomatoes, preferably fire-roasted

1 (15-ounce) can lentils, drained and rinsed, or 1½ to 2 cups cooked

2 teaspoons good-quality curry powder, or to taste

5 to 6 ounces baby spinach

¼ to ½ cup chopped fresh cilantro

¼ cup raisins, optional

Salt and freshly ground pepper, to taste

1. Cook the pasta according to the package directions until al dente, then drain.

2. Meanwhile, heat the oil in a large saucepan. Add the onions and garlic, and sauté over medium-low heat until golden, stirring frequently, about 5 minutes. Add the bell peppers and sauté for 2 to 3 minutes longer.

3. Add the tomatoes, lentils, and curry powder. Bring to a gentle simmer, then cover and cook over medium-low heat for 5 minutes.

4. Add the spinach, in batches, and cook briefly, covered, until just wilted but still bright green.

5. Stir in the cilantro and the raisins, if using, and remove from the heat.

6. Combine the cooked pasta with the lentil mixture in a large serving bowl and toss gently. Season with salt and pepper, toss again, and serve at once.

Kale Pesto Pasta with Mushroom Bacon

6 servings

When making pesto, kale goes a lot further than the traditional ingredient, basil. And to my palate, it's even better. It retains its bright color and offers more bang for the nutritional buck. Here, the lovely green color gets an additional boost with a small amount of green peas. And to please basil lovers, this recipe offers the option of adding a small quantity, instead of parsley or cilantro. Smoky-sweet mushroom bacon gives this dish great little bursts of flavor.

1 pound pasta (any short chunky shape)

FOR THE KALE PESTO

1 bunch kale (about 8 ounces), lacinato or curly

1 tablespoon olive oil

3 to 4 cloves garlic, minced

1 cup frozen (thawed) green peas

Juice of ½ lemon (2 tablespoons)

¼ to ½ cup fresh basil, cilantro, or parsley leaves

⅓ cup walnuts, optional

Salt and freshly ground pepper, to taste

Dried hot red pepper flakes to taste, optional

Mushroom Bacon (page 195 and see Note)

Easiest Vegan Parmesan (page 87) for topping, optional

1. Cook the pasta according to the package directions until al dente, then drain and return to the cooking pot.

2. Meanwhile, make the kale pesto: Rinse the kale and slice thinly, right through the stem. You can slice a few leaves at a time, or even the whole bunch if you're using lacinato.

3. Heat the oil in a skillet or stir-fry pan. Add the garlic and sauté until golden, about 2 minutes.

4. Add the kale and a little water, and cover. Steam until the kale wilts down and is tender, but still bright green, 3 to 5 minutes.

5. Transfer the kale mixture to a food processor, along with the remaining pesto ingredients and ½ cup of water. Pulse until evenly and finely chopped. If needed, add a little more water so that the mixture flows a bit, but remains thick.

6. Combine the pesto with the cooked and drained pasta in the cooking pot. If necessary, add a little more water to distribute the pesto. Season with salt and pepper, and the dried hot red pepper flakes, if using. Serve at once, topping each portion with some Mushroom Bacon, and the Vegan Parmesan, if desired.

NOTE

If you love the idea of bacon-flavored mushrooms, double the Mushroom Bacon recipe. You won't regret it!

Spinach Pesto Pasta
with Potatoes

6 servings

Pasta with pesto, potatoes, and green beans is a rustic Italian classic—from Genoa, to be exact. It may seem odd to combine pasta and potatoes, but it works amazingly well. It's carb heaven, perhaps, but still healthy and extra hearty, packed as it is with spinach and herbs.

FOR THE SPINACH PESTO

5 to 6 ounces fresh baby spinach

¼ cup fresh parsley leaves

¼ cup fresh basil leaves (or just use ½ cup parsley)

2 scallions, green parts only, coarsely chopped

1 tablespoon lemon juice

1 tablespoon olive oil

¼ cup walnuts, optional

4 medium red-skinned potatoes

10 to 12 ounces pasta (any short chunky shape)

1 tablespoon olive oil

3 to 4 cloves garlic, minced

8 to 10 ounces fresh green beans, trimmed and cut into 1-inch lengths, or (thawed) frozen green beans

Salt and freshly ground pepper, to taste

Easiest Vegan Parmesan (page 87), optional

1. Combine all the ingredients for the pesto in a food processor with ¼ cup of water and pulse until evenly and finely chopped. If needed, add a little more water so that the mixture flows a bit, but remains thick.

2. Scrub the potatoes and cook or microwave them just until done. When they're cool enough to handle, cut them into 1-inch dice and set them aside.

3. Cook the pasta according to the package directions until al dente, then drain.

4. Meanwhile, heat the oil in a large skillet. Add the garlic and sauté over low heat until golden. Add about ¼ cup of water, along with the green beans, and steam, covered, until tender-crisp.

5. Combine the cooked pasta, potatoes, and green bean mixture (including any remaining liquid) in a large serving bowl. Add the pesto and toss gently until combined well. Season to taste with salt and pepper and toss again. Serve at once. Pass around the Easiest Vegan Parmesan, if using.

Easiest Vegan Parmesan

Makes ¾ cup

Many of the pasta recipes in this chapter call for this tasty topping, so you'll want to have plenty on hand. Luckily, it just takes a few minutes to throw together. While most homemade versions combine nutritional yeast with ground cashews or almonds, this one offers the shortcut of using almond flour (found in most natural foods stores) instead of having to grind down the nuts. This eliminates the use of a food processor, so it saves time and energy.

Now it is true that neither almond flour nor nutritional yeast are particularly cheap, but they're sold in quantities that will allow you to make this recipe many times over. Ready-made vegan Parmesan comes in 4- to 8-ounce containers and, by weight, is many times pricier.

The other good news is that a tablespoon or two of nutritional yeast gives you a good dose of vitamin B12, a valuable and hard-to-get vitamin in a plant-based diet without supplementation. And, almond flour is a great source of vitamin E and calcium.

½ cup almond flour

¼ cup nutritional yeast

¼ teaspoon salt

1. Combine all the ingredients in a small bowl and stir together until well combined.

2. Store any unused portion in an airtight container in the refrigerator, where it will keep for several weeks.

Italian-Style Sausage & Peppers Pasta

6 to 8 servings

This home-style Italian standard makes a warming one-dish meal that's ideal for cool weather. Vegan sausage might seem like a splurge ingredient, but when you consider how much protein it adds to the dish—20 grams per link, in the case of most brands—it's a nutritional bargain. Any short pasta shape works here, but it's especially good with twists, like gemelli, rotini, or fusilli. A tossed salad is all you need to complete the meal, but adding a steamed green vegetable (broccoli, green beans, Brussels sprouts, etc.) never hurts!

2 tablespoons olive oil, divided

1 (14-ounce) package (4 links) vegan sausage, cut into ½-inch slices

1 pound pasta (any short shape)

1 large onion, quartered and thinly sliced

2 to 3 cloves garlic, minced

2 medium bell peppers (any color), cut into strips

1 (28-ounce) can crushed tomatoes

2 teaspoons Italian seasoning

¼ teaspoon dried red pepper flakes, or to taste (optional)

Salt and freshly ground pepper, to taste

¼ cup chopped fresh parsley or basil, or to taste

Easiest Vegan Parmesan (page 87), optional

1. Heat 1 tablespoon of the oil in a large skillet or stir-fry pan. Add the sausage and cook over medium-high heat, stirring often, until most sides are golden brown. Transfer to a plate or bowl and set aside. Wipe out the skillet to reuse.

2. Meanwhile, cook the pasta according to the package directions until al dente, then drain.

3. Heat the remaining tablespoon of oil in the pan you used to cook the sausage. Add the onions and sauté over medium heat until translucent.

4. Add the garlic and peppers and continue to sauté for 4 to 5 minutes, or until all are soft and turning golden.

5. Stir in the tomatoes and the Italian seasoning. Bring the sauce to a simmer, then cover and cook, over low heat, for 5 minutes.

6. Combine the pasta, sausage, and tomato sauce in a large serving bowl or in the pasta pot.

7. Season with the red pepper flakes, if using, salt (you may not need much, if any), and pepper. Stir in the fresh herb, or pass it around for topping, and serve at once. Pass around the Easiest Vegan Parmesan for topping, if desired.

Pasta Carbonara
with Broccoli & Vegan Bacon

6 servings

Carbonara refers to a dish made with bacon. In this vegan twist on a traditional Italian pasta dish, you have a choice of using homemade tempeh bacon or mushroom bacon— or you can go the route of prepared vegan bacon. Either way, the briny bites add lots of flavor to an otherwise mild dish. A simple salad of tomatoes, chickpeas, and bell peppers would make a great side dish.

1 pound pasta (your favorite shape)

Tempeh Bacon (page 196), Mushroom Bacon (page 195), or one 6- to 8-ounce package vegan bacon (your favorite brand)

6 cups finely chopped broccoli florets

3 to 4 cloves garlic, minced

1 to 2 tablespoons olive oil

⅓ cup Easiest Vegan Parmesan (page 87), optional

¼ cup chopped fresh parsley

Salt and freshly ground pepper, to taste

1. Cook the pasta according to the package directions until al dente, then drain.

2. Prepare the vegan bacon of your choice in a large skillet, then transfer to a plate. If you've chosen tempeh bacon, cut it into small bits.

3. Combine the broccoli and garlic with about ½ cup of water in the same pan that you used to cook the vegan bacon. Cover and steam until the broccoli is bright green and tender-crisp. Remove from the heat.

4. Combine the cooked pasta, vegan bacon, and broccoli mixture in a serving bowl. Drizzle in some olive oil. Add the Easiest Vegan Parmesan, if using, and parsley, and toss well. Season with salt and pepper and serve.

Vegan on a Budget

Noodles with Spicy Peanut Sauce

6 servings

The basic components of this dish—ordinary pasta combined with tomatoes and zucchini, get their yum factor (along with an Asian spin) from a luscious peanut sauce. Truth be told, Thai peanut sauce (sometimes labeled peanut satay) can be more economical to buy (especially store brands) than to make from scratch. But I like to give options, so feel free to choose.

10 to 12 ounces linguine or spaghetti

1 medium or 2 small zucchini, sliced

2 medium tomatoes, diced

2 to 3 scallions, thinly sliced

1 cup bottled Thai peanut sauce, or Coconut Peanut Sauce or Dressing (page 203), or more, to taste

1 teaspoon hot sauce, such as sriracha, or to taste

Salt and freshly ground pepper, to taste

Fresh cilantro leaves for garnish, optional

Peanut halves for garnish, optional

1. Cook the pasta according to the package directions until al dente, then drain.

2. Meanwhile, combine the zucchini, tomatoes, and scallions in a medium skillet with ¼ cup water. Cover and steam until the zucchini is just tender-crisp and the tomato has softened, about 3 to 4 minutes.

3. Combine the cooked noodles with the peanut sauce in a large serving bowl and stir until evenly coated. Add enough hot sauce to please your palate, but don't go overboard—you can always pass it around to let everyone add more to their own taste. Season with salt and pepper.

4. Top each serving with some of the zucchini-tomato mixture and garnish with cilantro and/or peanuts, if desired.

Stir-Fried Noodles with Cabbage & Corn

4 servings

This quick noodle dish, one of my longtime favorites, features two economical vegetables—cabbage and corn. It pairs well with a simple protein preparation, like Savory & Sweet Sautéed Tofu or Seitan (page 194). Serve with a platter of raw veggies for color and crunch.

8 ounces spaghetti or linguine (see Variation)

2 tablespoons safflower or another neutral vegetable oil

6 cups thinly sliced green cabbage or bagged coleslaw

2 cups fresh or (thawed) frozen corn kernels

4 scallions, sliced

1 tablespoon grated fresh or squeeze-bottle ginger

2 tablespoons soy sauce or tamari, or to taste

Sriracha or another hot sauce, or dried hot red pepper flakes, to taste

Freshly ground pepper, to taste

1. Cook the noodles according to the package directions until al dente, then drain.

2. Meanwhile, heat the oil in a wide skillet or stir-fry pan. Add the cabbage, corn, scallions, and ginger, and stir-fry over medium-high heat until the cabbage is slightly wilted but still crisp, about 3 to 5 minutes.

3. Stir in the cooked noodles, then season with soy sauce, hot sauce, and pepper. Serve at once.

VARIATION

- For a small splurge and to make this recipe more authentic, use Chinese wheat noodles, udon noodles, or soba noodles, instead of the spaghetti or linguine.

Teriyaki Asian Noodles
with Stir-Fried Tofu & Vegetables

4 servings

Here's an Asian-inspired noodle dish that's a cousin to chow mein. This one uses different vegetables and is made heartier with tofu. Serve one of the Simple Slaws (page 137) for a nice meal.

1 medium red (or any color) bell pepper, cut into narrow strips

6 ounces mushrooms (any variety), cleaned, stemmed, and sliced

4 to 6 ounces slender green beans, trimmed, or frozen (thawed) green beans

2 to 3 scallions, sliced

8 ounces spaghetti or linguine (see Variation)

1 (14-ounce) tub extra-firm tofu

1½ tablespoons neutral vegetable oil, such as safflower oil

¼ cup homemade Teriyaki Marinade (page 199) or bottled teriyaki marinade, plus more for serving

2 teaspoons grated fresh or squeeze-bottle ginger

Freshly ground pepper, to taste

Sesame seeds or chopped toasted peanuts or cashews for topping, optional

Sriracha or another hot seasoning, optional

1. Prepare the bell peppers, mushrooms, green beans, and scallions as directed (once you've got the noodles and tofu started, the recipe goes very fast). Set aside.

2. Cook the noodles according to the package directions until al dente, then drain.

3. Meanwhile, cut the tofu into 6 slabs crosswise and blot very well with clean tea towels or paper towels. (Or, better yet, if you have a tofu press, press the tofu ahead of time.) Cut into dice.

4. Heat the oil in a stir-fry pan. Add the tofu and stir-fry over medium-high heat, stirring often, until golden on most sides, 5 to 8 minutes.

5. Add the bell peppers, mushrooms, and green beans. Stir-fry for 2 to 3 minutes longer, just until the vegetables are tender-crisp. Stir in the scallions.

6. Add the cooked noodles to the pan, along with the teriyaki marinade, ginger, and pepper. Stir-fry just until everything is combined well and piping hot. Add more teriyaki marinade to taste, if desired.

7. Sprinkle some of the sesame seeds or nuts, if using, on top of the dish or pass them around. Serve at once straight from the pan. passing around teriyaki marinade and the hot seasoning, if using, for individual servings.

Vegetable Chow Mein

4 servings

Chow mein is a wholly American invention, as far as I can tell, and it's been a staple on Asian menus for decades. Don't call for takeout when it's so easy to make this at home, especially since the vegetables outweigh the noodles in this version. A perfect companion to this dish is Savory & Sweet Sautéed Tofu or Seitan (page 194). Add a platter of cherry tomatoes and baby carrots, and you've got a great meal.

8 ounces spaghetti or linguine (see Variation)

2 tablespoons safflower or another high-heat oil

1 large onion, quartered and sliced

3 large stalks celery or bok choy, sliced on a diagonal

1 medium broccoli crown, cut into bite-sized florets

1 red bell pepper, cut into narrow strips

6 to 8 ounces cremini (baby bella) or white mushrooms, cleaned, stemmed, and sliced

2 to 3 scallions, white and green parts, optional

2 tablespoons soy sauce or tamari, or more, to taste

Freshly ground pepper, to taste

Dried hot red pepper flakes or hot sauce for serving, optional

1. Cook the noodles according to the package directions until al dente, then drain.

2. Meanwhile, before starting the stir-fry, have all the vegetables cut and ready.

3. Heat the oil in a stir-fry pan. Add the onion and sauté over medium heat until translucent, about 4 to 5 minutes.

4. Add the cooked noodles to the pan, turn up the heat, and stir-fry until they're lightly browned here and there.

5. Add the celery, broccoli, bell peppers, and mushrooms, and stir-fry over high heat until all are just tender-crisp. Stir in the scallions.

6. Remove from the heat. Season with soy sauce and lots of pepper. Serve at once, passing around extra soy sauce as well as the hot red pepper flakes or hot sauce, if desired.

VARIATION

For a small splurge, try using Chinese wheat noodles, udon noodles, or soba noodles instead of the spaghetti or linguine.

Vegan on a Budget

Yellow Curry Rice Noodles

4 servings

Inspired by a dish known as "Singapore Noodles," this recipe combines Asian and Indian influences. This tasty and pleasantly offbeat dish is seasoned with both soy sauce and curry. Inexpensive rice noodles are a nice change of pace from regular pasta and are widely available in the Asian foods section of most supermarkets. For this recipe, make sure to get rice-stick noodles, also known as rice vermicelli, rather than the wide rice noodles used for making Pad Thai. This one-dish meal can be completed with any kind of simple salad.

8 ounces rice-stick noodles (rice vermicelli)

1 large onion, quartered and thinly sliced

2 cloves garlic, minced

1 cup baby carrots, halved (if thin) or quartered lengthwise

1 red bell pepper, cut into narrow, 2-inch-long strips

1 green bell pepper, cut into narrow, 2-inch-long strips

1 tablespoon neutral vegetable oil, such as safflower oil

1 (8-ounce) package baked tofu, cut into narrow strips

1 cup frozen green peas, thawed

SAUCE

¼ cup soy sauce or tamari

1 teaspoon natural granulated sugar

2 teaspoons good-quality curry powder

2 teaspoons grated fresh or squeeze-bottle ginger, to taste

1. Combine all the ingredients for the sauce with ¼ cup of water in a small bowl, then whisk together. Set aside until needed.

2. Cook the noodles according to the package directions, then drain. Transfer to a cutting board and chop in several directions to shorten.

3. Meanwhile, prepare the vegetables as directed before beginning to stir-fry.

4. Heat the oil in a large skillet or stir-fry pan. Add the onions, garlic, and carrots, and stir-fry over medium-high heat for 4 minutes. Add the red and green bell peppers and tofu strips and stir-fry for 3 to 4 minutes longer.

5. Add the cooked noodles to the pan, along with the sauce and peas. Toss quickly and stir-fry just until everything is well heated through. Serve at once.

5

PLANT-BASED BLISS ON BREAD: SANDWICHES, BURGERS & PIZZAS

When people go plant-based, they often worry that they'll miss the kind of crave-worthy preparations highlighted in this chapter. Not only is that untrue, but it's easy to make healthier, plant-based versions of these favorites in your kitchen. This chapter will offer a selection of hefty sandwiches; burger recipes based on beans and grains; and a few offbeat pizzas. Not only can you keep these kinds of comfort classics in your culinary repertoire, you can enjoy them more often—guilt free, and inexpensively.

Avocado & Chickpea Sandwich Spread

Makes about 2 cups, enough for about 8 slices of bread

Pairing the great flavors of avocado and chickpeas, this tasty sandwich spread isn't merely avocado toast. I hope you'll find it as addictive as I do. Using a very fresh multigrain bread makes it even better. If you have a pot of soup on the stove and want to serve it with more than plain bread, this just might be what you're looking for.

1 medium ripe avocado

1 (15-ounce) can chickpeas, drained and rinsed

¼ cup vegan mayonnaise, or to taste

1 teaspoon prepared mustard

2 to 3 tablespoons lemon juice, or to taste

Pinch of cumin

Salt and freshly ground pepper, to taste

Fresh whole grain bread, as needed

OPTIONAL GARNISHES (USE ONE OR TWO)

Sunflower seeds

Finely chopped black olives

Finely diced fresh tomato

Thinly sliced scallions (green part only)

Finely chopped fresh parsley or cilantro

1. Cut the avocado in half, and remove the pit. Scoop the flesh out into a shallow bowl.

2. Add the chickpeas. Mash with a large fork until fairly smooth, leaving a bit of texture.

3. Add the mayonnaise, mustard, lemon juice, and cumin, and stir until combined well. Season lightly with salt and pepper.

4. Spread the avocado and chickpea mixture on fresh bread, allowing 1 or 2 slices per serving. Top with any of the desired toppings. Serve at once.

Hummus Wraps
with Greens & Avocado

Makes 2 wraps

This recipe is designed to make two generous wraps, but you can halve it to make just one, or double it for four. The Homemade Hummus (page 200) will have you covered, even if you double the recipe. The wraps easily can be transported to school or work in a crushproof container, or serve them for dinner with soup or with baked sweet potatoes.

2 (10-inch) wraps, preferably whole grain

Homemade Hummus (page 200), as needed

1 small avocado, peeled and thinly sliced

1 medium firm tomato, thinly sliced

A big handful of baby spinach or arugula or baby power greens per wrap

1. Lay 1 wrap on a large plate or cutting board. Spread ½ cup of hummus over the surface.

2. Arrange half of the avocado slices and half of the tomato slices down the center of the wrap over the hummus. Top with half of the greens.

3. Fold 2 opposite sides of the wrap over the vegetables, then roll up snugly, making sure the sides stay tucked in. Cut the wrap in half with a sharp knife.

4. Make and cut another wrap in the same manner and serve.

NOTES

Baked tofu comes in 5-ounce and 8-ounce packages. Use a full 5-ounce package or half of an 8-ounce package.

For the vegan salad dressing, use whatever dressing you have on hand, or even vegan mayo. I wouldn't recommend something runny or oily, like vinaigrette, however. Tartar Dressing or Dip (page 199) is quite good to use for these wraps.

Baked Tofu Wraps with Apple & Greens

Makes 2 wraps

The surprising pop of tart green apple makes these wraps especially tasty. These are a treat to take to work or school, packed up in a crushproof container. Or, keep them in mind for a quick at-home lunch, or for dinner with soup or a simple potato or sweet potato dish. The recipe can be halved to make just one wrap, or doubled to make four.

2 (10-inch, good-quality) wraps

2 big handfuls of baby spinach or arugula or baby power greens per wrap

Vegan salad dressing of your choice, as needed (see Notes)

4 to 5 ounces baked tofu (any variety; see Notes), cut into thin strips

½ Granny Smith or another crisp, tart apple, thinly sliced

½ small or ¼ medium avocado, or as needed, peeled and thinly sliced

1. Lay the wraps on a cutting board.

2. Combine the greens with some vegan salad dressing in a small mixing bowl and toss together until evenly coated. Spread a little more dressing on the surface of the wraps.

3. Place half of the greens just to the side of center of 1 wrap, then arrange half of the tofu, apple, and avocado in another row just to the other side of center.

4. Fold 2 opposite sides of the wrap over the vegetables, then roll up snugly, making sure the sides stay tucked in. Cut in half with a sharp knife.

5. Complete and cut the second wrap in the same manner and serve.

Portobello & Seitan Cheesesteak Sandwiches

Makes 3 or 4 sandwiches

Some variations of vegan cheesesteak sandwiches use seitan, while others use portobello mushrooms. I think combining the two—a great blend of meatiness and umami—makes these hefty sandwiches even better. Quick to put together, these sandwiches make a nice fast dinner, served with a simple salad.

1 tablespoon olive oil

1 medium onion, quartered and thinly sliced

1 medium bell pepper (any color), cut into strips

8 ounces Homemade Seitan (page 192), or packaged, cut into strips

2 portobello mushrooms, cleaned, stemmed, and cut into strips

1½ cups vegan mozzarella cheese shreds

3 to 4 hero rolls, preferably whole grain

Sriracha or another hot sauce, optional

1. Heat the oil in a medium skillet. Add the onions and sauté over medium-low heat until golden.

2. Add the bell peppers, seitan, and mushrooms. Turn the heat up to medium-high and sauté until everything is sizzling hot and touched with light brown spots, about 5 to 7 minutes.

3. Stir in the vegan mozzarella and cook just until it starts to melt.

4. Divide the filling among the hero rolls (you can hollow them out a bit if you'd like, so that more of the filling can go in). This will fill 3 or 4 hero rolls, depending on how large they are. Cut each sandwich in half and serve at once, passing around your favorite hot sauce, if desired.

Vegan on a Budget

Barbecue-Flavored Lentil Sloppy Joes

6 servings

As satisfying as any kind of burger, these barbecue-flavored lentil sloppy joes come together in minutes if you have lentils cooked and ready. There's also the option of using canned lentils, because many of us, including yours truly, never seem to remember to cook them ahead of time. Not that they take as long as other legumes, but still, canned lentils save you that valuable 30 to 40 minutes when you need to get a meal on the table. Sautéed golden potatoes and a green vegetable, plus some diced small tomatoes, make nice accompaniments. Or, just serve with a platter of raw veggies and a dip.

2 teaspoons olive oil

1 medium onion, finely chopped

2 cloves garlic, minced

6 to 8 ounces cremini (baby bella) or white mushrooms, cleaned, stemmed, and chopped

2 (15-ounce) cans lentils, drained and rinsed, or 3 cups cooked (see How to Cook Lentils, page xvii)

1 cup bottled barbecue sauce (your favorite natural variety) or Super-Quick No-Cook BBQ Sauce, plus more, as needed

Freshly ground pepper, to taste

Dried hot red pepper flakes or sriracha to taste, optional

Burger buns, small ciabatta breads, or English muffins, to serve

1. Heat the oil in a large skillet. Add the onions and the garlic, and sauté over medium-low heat until both are golden, about 3 to 4 minutes.

2. Add the mushrooms. Cover and cook over medium heat until wilted, about 3 to 4 minutes.

3. Add the lentils, barbecue sauce, a few grindings of pepper, and the hot red pepper flakes or sriracha, if desired.

4. Bring to a simmer, then cook over low heat, uncovered, for 10 minutes, or until everything is piping hot. The liquid should be thickened and enveloping the lentils and mushrooms nicely. If you'd like the mixture to be saucier, add ¼ to ½ cup more barbecue sauce.

5. For each serving, spoon some of the filling onto the bread of your choice and serve open face.

Barbecue-Flavored
Tofu Subs

4 to 6 servings

Barbecue sauce is one of the best flavorings for tofu, as you'll see when you try these big, bold tofu sandwiches. I like to complement this meal with fresh corn and a salad or a Simple Slaw (page 137).

1 (14-ounce) tub firm or extra-firm tofu

2 tablespoons olive oil, divided

1 large onion, quartered and thinly sliced

1 bell pepper (any color), cut into short narrow strips

¾ cup bottled barbecue sauce, your favorite natural variety, or Super-Quick No-Cook Barbecue Sauce (page 202), plus more, as needed

Freshly ground pepper, to taste

4 large soft whole grain round or hero rolls, or 1 long baguette (see Note)

1. Cut the tofu into 6 slabs crosswise. Blot well on paper towels or clean tea towels. Cut each slab into ½-inch dice.

2. Heat 1 tablespoon of oil in a medium skillet or stir-fry pan. Add the onions and sauté over medium heat until translucent. Add the bell peppers and continue to sauté until the onions are golden. Transfer the mixture to a bowl, cover, and set aside.

3. Heat the remaining tablespoon of oil in the same skillet. Add the tofu and sauté over medium-high heat, stirring frequently until golden on most sides.

4. Pour ½ cup of the barbecue sauce into the skillet, and stir to coat the tofu. Cook for 5 to 8 minutes, or until the sauce reduces. Pour in the remaining ¼ cup of sauce and cook for a minute or two longer. Season with pepper.

5. Slice the bread in half horizontally with a serrated knife. Divide the tofu mixture among the bottoms of the bread, then top with the onion and bell pepper mixture. Cover with the tops of the bread, or, leave open face and serve.

NOTE

If you use a baguette, choose one that's not too skinny and, preferably, whole grain. Cut it into 4 sections and split open.

VARIATION

- The barbecue-flavored tofu can also be served over rice if you prefer it to bread, or even on its own.

Homemade Vegan Burgers

With all the great vegan burgers on the market these days, what's the advantage of making them at home? Well, for starters, there's the cost. Most vegan burgers come in two- or four-packs, and while that's more economical than going out for a burger dinner, what if you're feeding a larger crowd? Or what if you want to do some batch cooking for the freezer? Is there someone in your household who has a bigger appetite and wants to have seconds? That's where homemade burgers come in handy. The recipes that follow were developed with the busy cook in mind, too. The food processor takes care of the chopping, and shortcuts, like bottled spices and herb blends, eliminate the need for measuring tons of spices.

And while you've got the burgers in the oven, remember that the ideal accompaniment, Easy Oven Fries (page 66), can bake along at the same time.

Vegan burgers welcome the same kind of toppings and embellishments as their meaty counterparts. Here are some ideas.

Serving Suggestions for Vegan Burgers

- Guacamole or avocado slices
- Red onion slices
- Browned onions
- Roasted red peppers
- Wilted mushrooms
- Vegan Bacon (page 195–196, with tempeh or mushroom variations) or packaged
- Fresh sprouts
- Sliced tomatoes
- Shredded lettuce or mixed greens

Condiments

- Ketchup and mustard, of course
- Vegan mayo (stir in a little sriracha for some spice)
- Tartar Dressing or Dip (page 199)

Breads

- Whole grain burger buns
- English muffins
- Kaiser rolls
- Pita bread

Salsa
Black Bean Burgers

Makes 6 large or 8 to 9 smaller burgers

These hearty burgers were inspired by my friend and colleague Laura Theodore (The Jazzy Vegetarian—that's her brand, though she's a longtime vegan). Her "Hungry Guy" burgers, using only five ingredients, proved to me that homemade vegan burgers don't need a million ingredients and lots of steps to be really good. These burgers, and the burger recipes that follow, all keep to the formula of using a can of legumes and a cup or so of a flavor-boosting ingredient.

---

1 (15-ounce) can black beans, drained, liquid reserved

1 cup oatmeal (quick-cooking rolled oats)

⅔ cup fine breadcrumbs or ⅓ cup chickpea flour

1 cup salsa (your favorite variety)

1 to 2 scallions, thinly sliced

1 tablespoon barbecue seasoning (for more information, see page xxii)

Freshly ground pepper, to taste

1. Preheat the oven to 375°F and line a roasting pan or baking sheet with parchment paper.

2. Combine all the ingredients, except for the cooking oil spray, in a food processor and pulse until evenly and finely chopped. Stop the machine to stir once or twice, scraping down the sides as needed. Add a bit of the reserved bean liquid if the chopped mixture is too dry.

3. To form the burgers, use a ⅓-cup measuring cup for smaller burgers; ½-cup measuring cup for larger burgers. Spray the inside of the cup with cooking oil spray or

spread a little oil in the measuring cup with a paper towel.

4. Use the measuring cup to scoop up the bean mixture, leveling it off but not packing it in too tightly. Invert the cup onto the parchment-lined roasting pan with a sharp tap to release the mixture. Repeat until the bean mixture is used up.

5. Spray the bottom of the measuring cup that you used to form the burgers and use it to flatten each burger to about a ½-inch thickness. Wipe the bottom of the cup and spray it from time to time.

6. Bake the burgers for 15 minutes, or until the bottoms are golden, then carefully flip and bake for 8 to 10 minutes longer. (Watch carefully to avoid overbaking and letting the burgers get dried out.)

7. Remove the burgers from the oven and let them stand for 5 minutes. Serve with desired toppings (see Serving Suggestions for Vegan Burgers, page 111).

Lentil-Walnut Burgers

Makes 6 large or 8 to 9 smaller burgers

Lentils and walnuts make a good team in these hearty burgers, each supplying their unique flavor as well as plenty of protein. Walnuts, while relatively affordable compared with other nuts, are a bit of a splurge ingredient, but you don't need many here. They're well worth it for their rich flavor and beneficial nutrients, including omega-3 fatty acids. (Try to buy them in bulk if you're using them in larger quantities.)

⅔ cup walnut pieces

1 (15-ounce) can lentils, drained but not rinsed, or 1½ cups cooked lentils (page xvii), with a little of their cooking liquid

⅔ cup whole grain breadcrumbs or ⅓ cup chickpea flour

1 cup oatmeal (quick-cooking oats)

¼ cup good-quality ketchup

¼ cup teriyaki marinade

1 tablespoon dried onion flakes

1 tablespoon barbecue seasoning (for more information, see page xxii)

Freshly ground pepper, to taste

1. Preheat the oven to 375°F and line a roasting pan or baking sheet with parchment paper.

2. Place the walnuts in a food processor fitted with the metal blade and pulse until they're finely ground.

3. Add the remaining ingredients, except for the cooking oil spray, to the food processor, and pulse until everything is well combined. Stop the machine to stir once or twice, scraping down the sides as needed. (If you're using cooked lentils, add a bit of the cooking liquid if the mixture seems dry.)

4. To form the burgers, use a ⅓-cup measuring cup for smaller burgers; ½-cup measuring cup for larger burgers. Spray the inside of the cup with cooking oil spray or spread a little oil in the measuring cup with a paper towel.

5. Use the measuring cup to scoop up the bean mixture, leveling it off but not packing it in too tightly. Invert the cup onto the parchment-lined roasting pan with a sharp tap to release the mixture. Repeat until the bean mixture is used up.

6. Spray the bottom of the measuring cup that you used to form the burgers, and use it to flatten each burger to about a ½-inch thickness. Wipe the bottom of the cup and spray it from time to time.

7. Bake the burgers for 15 minutes, or until the bottoms are golden, then carefully flip and bake for 8 to 10 minutes longer. (Watch carefully to avoid overbaking and letting the burgers get dried out.)

8. Remove the burgers from the oven and let them stand for 5 minutes. Serve with desired toppings (see Serving Suggestions for Vegan Burgers, page 111).

Curried Chickpea Burgers

Makes 6 large or 8 to 9 smaller burgers

As you know by now, Indian simmer sauce is one of my favorite shortcuts, and since it is especially compatible with chickpeas, it is brought into service here. Try the tomato and coconut-based Jalfrezi variety for a fantastic flavor boost. Tartar Dressing or Dip (page 199) is an especially good embellishment for these burgers, but feel free to use your favorite condiments.

1 (15-ounce) can chickpeas, drained and rinsed

1 cup Indian simmer sauce (see Note)

1 cup oatmeal (quick-cooking oats)

1 cup fresh whole grain breadcrumbs or ½ cup chickpea flour

2 big handfuls of baby spinach or other baby greens, lightly wilted

2 scallions, green parts only, roughly chopped

1 tablespoon lemon juice

1 tablespoon olive oil (for extra richness), optional

Salt and freshly ground pepper, to taste

1. Preheat the oven to 375°F and line a roasting pan or baking sheet with parchment paper.

2. Combine all the ingredients, except for the cooking oil spray, in a food processor and pulse until evenly and finely chopped. Stop the machine to stir once or twice, scraping down the sides as needed.

3. To form the burgers, use a ⅓-cup measuring cup for smaller burgers; ½-cup measuring cup for larger burgers. Spray the inside of the cup with cooking oil spray or spread a little oil in the measuring cup with a paper towel.

4. Use the measuring cup to scoop up the bean mixture, leveling it off but not packing it in too tightly. Invert the cup onto the parchment-lined roasting pan with a sharp tap to release the mixture. Repeat until the bean mixture is used up.

5. Spray the bottom of the measuring cup that you used to form the burgers, and use it to flatten each burger to about a ½-inch thickness. Wipe the bottom of the cup and spray it from time to time.

6. Bake the burgers for 15 minutes, or until the bottoms are golden, then carefully flip and bake for 8 to 10 minutes longer. (Watch carefully to avoid overbaking and letting the burgers get dried out.)

NOTE

Look for Indian simmer sauces in the international foods aisles in supermarkets and in natural foods stores. They come in a range of vegan options from mild to spicy, including Goan coconut, Kashmir curry, Jalfrezi, and Madras curry. Some include dairy, so be sure to check labels.

VARIATIONS

■ If you don't care to make your own mushroom bacon, use a prepared vegan bacon product. About 5 or 6 strips should be about right; chop into small pieces and cook on a lightly oiled skillet until browned and crisp on most sides.

■ Use about half a cup of chopped briny black olives instead of the mushroom bacon. This combination is inspired by the classic pizza Niçoise.

Pizza with Caramelized Onions & Mushroom Bacon

Makes 6 slices

Here's a no-tomato pizza whose big flavor comes from slow-cooked onions and smoky homemade mushroom bacon. This pizza tends to vanish quickly, so I'd suggest doubling the recipe if you have a crowd of hungry eaters.

1½ tablespoons olive oil

2 large or 3 medium onions, quartered and thinly sliced

Mushroom Bacon (page 195)

1½ cups vegan mozzarella or pepper jack cheese shreds, or a combination

1 (12-to 14-inch) packaged pizza crust or two large flatbread pizza crusts

1. Heat the oil in a skillet or stir-fry pan. Add the onions and cook slowly over low heat, stirring often, until soft and very lightly browned, about 15 minutes. Transfer to a plate.

2. Preheat the oven according to the pizza crust package directions (usually 425°F or 450°F).

3. While the oven is heating up, prepare the Mushroom Bacon in the same skillet you used to cook the onions.

4. Sprinkle the vegan cheese evenly over the surface of the pizza crust or crusts, followed by the caramelized onions, then the mushrooms.

5. Bake the pizza according to the pizza crust package directions (on a pan, a pizza stone, or right on the oven rack) until the cheese is melted and the crust is golden brown on the bottom. Once again, refer to the package directions to get a sense of the recommended baking time (usually about 10 minutes).

6. Remove the pizza from the oven and let it stand for a minute or two. Then cut it into wedges or sections to serve.

Red Onion, Mushroom & Kale Pizza

Makes 6 slices

Filling and tasty, this pizza departs only slightly from tradition—kale, not your usual pizza topping, works very well. As with all the pizza recipes in this chapter, this one is easy to double, and you won't regret it if you do!

1 tablespoon olive oil

½ medium red onion, quartered and thinly sliced

2 cloves garlic, minced, optional

1 cup cremini (baby bella) mushrooms, cleaned and sliced

½ cup marinara or pizza sauce, more or less as needed

1 (12- to 14-inch) pizza crust or two large flatbread pizza crusts

1 to 1½ cups vegan mozzarella or pepper jack cheese shreds, or a combination

1 to 2 big handfuls of baby kale leaves (see Note)

Dried hot red pepper flakes for topping, optional

1. Preheat the oven according to the pizza crust package directions (usually 425°F or 450°F).

2. Heat the oil in a medium skillet. Add the onions and garlic, if using, and sauté over medium-low heat until golden.

3. Add the mushrooms and continue to sauté until slightly wilted.

4. Spread the marinara or pizza sauce over the surface of the crust. Sprinkle the vegan cheese on evenly (using more or less cheese, depending on how cheesy you like your pizza), followed by the onion-mushroom mixture.

5. Bake the pizza according to the pizza crust package directions (on a pan, a pizza stone, or right on the oven rack) until the cheese is melted and the crust is golden brown on the bottom. Once again, refer to the package directions to get a sense of recommended time (usually about 10 minutes).

6. When the pizza is just about done, take it out of the oven and sprinkle a handful or two of baby kale leaves on top. Return it to the oven for just a minute or so, until the kale is wilted.

7. Remove the pizza from the oven and let it stand for a minute or two, then cut into 6 wedges or sections to serve.

NOTE

Feel free to use curly or lacinato kale if you have some on hand or baby kale is unavailable. Two to four leaves, depending on their size (and how much you love kale!) will do. Stem and chop into bite-sized pieces; rinse and dry. With a little olive oil on your palms, massage the kale for about 30 seconds.

Vegan Sausage & Peppers Pizza

Makes 6 slices

Sausage and peppers are a classic duo in Italian cuisine, so why not combine them for a flavorful and filling pizza, and, more importantly, why not make it vegan? I like to use Italian-style vegan sausage to keep the Italian spices authentic, but feel free to use another flavor.

In fact, use your creativity to vary this pizza. Start out by deciding if you want a classic red pizza or a white pizza (see Variations) and, if you'd like to add a little something special, go right ahead (see Optional Additions for ideas). This pizza disappears quickly even though it's so hearty, so I highly recommend doubling the recipe. All you need to make a complete meal is a colorful tossed salad.

2 teaspoons olive oil

1 link vegan sausage, sliced ¼ inch thick

½ green bell pepper, cut into narrow strips

½ red or yellow bell pepper, or a little of each, cut into narrow strips

½ cup pizza or marinara sauce, or as needed

1 (12- to 14-inch) packaged pizza crust, preferably whole grain

1 to 1½ cups vegan mozzarella or pepper jack cheese shreds, or a combination

Dried basil or oregano, or Italian seasoning (optional)

Dried hot red pepper flakes (optional)

1. Preheat the oven according to the pizza crust package directions (usually 425°F or 450°F).

2. Heat the oil in a medium skillet. Add the vegan sausage and all the bell peppers and sauté over medium heat for 5 minutes, stirring often.

3. Spread the pizza or marinara sauce over the surface of the crust. Distribute the cheese evenly, followed by the sausage and peppers mixture.

4. Bake the pizza according to the pizza crust package directions (on a pan, a pizza stone, or right on the oven rack) until the cheese is melted and the crust is golden brown on the bottom. Once again, refer to the package directions to get a sense of the recommended baking time (usually about 10 minutes).

5. Sprinkle with any of the optional toppings, then cut into 6 wedges to serve.

VARIATIONS

- To make white pizza, use pureed tofu instead of the pizza or marinara sauce as a base. Combine half of a 12.3-ounce container of firm or extra-firm silken tofu and a pinch of salt in a food processor and process until the mixture is completely smooth. Spread over the surface of the pizza crust. Don't overdo it—if there's too much (depending on the size of your crust), save the remainder of the pureed tofu for another use; it makes a nice base for salad dressing or can be stirred into almost any kind of soup.

- Use small broccoli florets instead of the bell peppers.

OPTIONAL ADDITIONS

- Artichoke hearts (marinated or not), quartered
- Strips of sun-dried tomatoes

Spinach & Olive Pizza

Makes 6 slices

Making your own pizza requires ideas more than exact recipes. This vegan spinach and olive pizza is a case in point. Once you've tried the tomato version, I recommend that you give the white pizza variation a try—the mellow tofu base contrasts nicely with the briny olives (see Variations). If you're feeding a hungry group, I highly recommend doubling both of these pizzas—they go down easy.

1 (12- to 14-inch) packaged good-quality pizza crust

½ cup pizza or marinara sauce, or as needed

1 to 1½ cups vegan mozzarella or pepper jack cheese shreds, or a combination

⅔ cup sliced black or green brine-cured olives, or a combination

2 big handfuls baby spinach

Sprinkling of dried oregano, Italian seasoning, and/or dried hot red pepper flakes, optional

Chopped or whole hot peppers from the olive bar, optional

1. Preheat the oven according to the pizza crust package directions (usually 425°F or 450°F).

2. Spread the crust with the marinara sauce, followed by the vegan cheese.

3. Bake the pizza according to the pizza crust package directions (on a pan, a pizza stone, or right on the oven rack) until the cheese is melted and the crust is golden brown on the bottom. Once again, refer to the package directions to get a sense of the recommended baking time (usually about 10 minutes).

4. Remove from the oven; sprinkle the olives on top, followed by the spinach. Return to the oven for no more than a minute, just until the spinach is wilted.

5. Top with any of the optional toppings, then cut into 6 wedges to serve.

VARIATIONS

- To make white pizza, use pureed tofu instead of the marinara sauce as a base. Combine half of a 12.3-ounce container of firm or extra-firm silken tofu and a pinch of salt in a food processor and process until the mixture is completely smooth. Spread over the surface of the pizza crust. Don't overdo it—if there's too much (depending on the size of your crust), save the remainder of the pureed tofu for another use; it makes a nice base for salad dressing or can be stirred into almost any kind of soup.

- Use baby arugula or baby power greens in place of the spinach.

Mini Tortilla Pizzas

4 servings as a main dish; 6 to 8 servings as an appetizer

These Southwestern-flavored mini pizzas, made with corn or flour tortillas, can be part of a satisfying meal, served with a salad that contains beans, like Potato Salad with Red Beans & Artichokes (page 139). These also make a fun appetizer, cut into smaller wedges.

1 (15-ounce) can vegan refried beans, mild or spicy

4 soft taco size (8-inch) corn or flour tortillas

1½ cups vegan cheddar shreds

½ bell pepper (any color), thinly sliced

1 cup cooked fresh or (thawed) frozen corn kernels

½ cup finely diced firm ripe tomato

1 small hot fresh chili pepper (like jalapeño), seeded and sliced

2 scallions, thinly sliced, or a handful of chopped cilantro

1. Preheat the oven to 400°F and line a baking sheet with parchment paper.

2. If the refried beans are too thick to spread, transfer them to a small bowl and stir in a little water.

3. Arrange the tortillas in a single layer on the parchment-lined baking sheet.

4. Spread a fairly thick layer of the refried beans over the surface of the tortillas (about ¼ cup per tortilla; any leftovers can be saved for another use).

5. Divide the remaining ingredients evenly over the tortillas in the order listed. Bake for 10 minutes, or until the cheese is bubbly and the tortillas firm up.

6. Remove from the oven, cut each tortilla into 4 wedges (kitchen shears are good for this), and serve.

SERIOUSLY FUN COOL DISHES & PLATTERS

Mention the word *salad* and, for some, it makes their eyes glaze over and their taste buds fall asleep. So, while it could be argued that most of the recipes in this chapter fit within the broad definition of *salad*, I made sure that they all have some luscious twist that will make them appeal to eaters of all stripes. Call them platters, composed dishes, or anything else you want: These aren't what skeptics would call "rabbit food."

Enjoy these fun, low-cost ways to make eating your "five a day" produce a reality. Beans, grains, plant proteins, and pastas, combined with vegetables, not only stretch the budget, but also exemplify what salad can be—cold food that's really comfort food.

Colorful Quinoa Protein Bowl

Makes 2 bowls

This quinoa bowl is an easy way to get your protein and veggies in one quick and colorful dish that serves as an entire meal. Edamame plays a leading role here (see Note). Beyond this recipe, keep them in mind as a great addition to soups or stews, or use them as a simple appetizer or snack on their own.

Your fun task here is to arrange the toppings artfully over cooked quinoa before passing around the dressing. You can double the recipe for more than two bowls, or cut it in half for just one, but I encourage you to make at least enough for two bowls, even if you're a solo eater. If you do so, arrange, cover, and refrigerate the extra portion(s)—you'll be glad it's waiting for you for tomorrow's dinner or portable lunch.

---

1 cup uncooked quinoa, rinsed

1 cup frozen edamame (fresh green soybeans), or see Variation

½ red bell pepper, cut into narrow strips

1 cup grated carrots (use pre-grated if you'd like)

Small quantity of toasted peanuts or cashews

Sesame-Ginger Dressing (page 198), or bottled, as needed

Scallions, optional

Sriracha or another hot seasoning, optional

1. Combine the quinoa with 2 cups of water in a small saucepan. Bring to a slow boil, then lower the heat, cover, and simmer for 15 minutes, or until the water is absorbed.

2. Meanwhile, combine the edamame with a small amount of water in a microwavable dish; cover and microwave until just done and warmed through. (Or, cook the edamame in a saucepan according to the package directions.)

3. When the quinoa is done, divide it between 2 roomy, shallow bowls. Arrange half of the edamame on each, followed by the bell pepper strips, carrots, and nuts.

4. Serve at once. Pass around the sesame-ginger dressing for drizzling on individual servings as well as the optional toppings, if desired.

NOTE

Edamame—fresh green soybeans—are available frozen and are a great protein value, at 10 to 12 grams per half cup. You'll find them in 8- to 16-ounce bags in the frozen vegetables section. It's best to buy them already shelled; they're easier to use that way, and also, why pay for the shells? Since you'll only be using 1 cup of them in this recipe (unless you decide to double it), store the rest of the edamame in the freezer for later use.

VARIATION

- Replace the edamame with any kind of bean you like. Chickpeas, black beans, or red beans work well in this recipe.

NOTE

This salad is great with almost any kind of dressing, so use whatever you've got on hand. If you'd like to use homemade dressing, the Basic Vinaigrette Dressing (page 197) works well or, for a creamy effect, try Tartar Dressing or Dip (page 199). Even plain vegan mayo, mixed with a little lemon juice, works well

VARIATION

■ This salad can be made with 8 ounces of baked tofu or seitan in place of tempeh. Cut the tofu into ½-inch dice and the seitan into small chunks and make croutons as directed in the first two steps.

Barbecue Tempeh Salad

4 servings

As a light meal, this delectable salad can stand on its own, especially for lunch. If you want to add something yummy on the side, Easy Oven Fries (page 66) are a great accompaniment. Or, simply serve with baked or microwaved sweet potatoes, just as they are—it's all good. For a nice midsummer meal, serve this salad with fresh corn on the cob instead of potatoes.

1 (8-ounce) package tempeh (any variety), or see Variation

1 tablespoon olive oil

½ cup Super-Quick No-Cook Barbecue Sauce (page 202) or bottled barbecue sauce

1 medium ripe avocado, peeled and diced

½ head romaine lettuce, coarsely shredded

2 big handfuls baby spinach

2 medium tomatoes, diced, or 1 cup halved cherry or grape tomatoes

1 cup grated carrots (use pre-grated, if you'd like)

Your favorite dressing, as needed (see Note)

1. Make the tempeh croutons: Cut the block of tempeh into ½-inch dice. Heat the olive oil in a skillet and sauté the tempeh over medium-high heat for 6 to 8 minutes, stirring often, until starting to turn golden.

2. Add about ½ cup of barbecue sauce to the tempeh and sauté until absorbed and the tempeh starts to brown. Add just a bit more sauce to coat, remove from the heat, and cover.

3. Combine the avocado, lettuce, baby spinach, tomatoes, and carrots in a salad bowl. Toss with your favorite dressing (or pass it around).

4. Divide the salad among 4 serving bowls or plates and top each with the warm tempeh croutons. Serve at once.

Salsa, Quinoa & Corn Salad

6 to 8 servings

Infused with the flavor of your favorite salsa, this abundant quinoa and corn salad packs in lots of other vegetables for a hearty meal in a bowl. And, since it's so sturdy and keeps well, it's also an excellent choice to share at potlucks all year round.

If you want to make this salad even heftier, see Optional Additions, or you can pair it with simple bean dishes or tortilla specialties using beans. Baked sweet potatoes and/or simply prepared broccoli, hardy greens, or green beans can be served on the side.

---

1 cup uncooked quinoa, rinsed (any color, or a combination of two)

1½ cups lightly cooked fresh or frozen corn kernels

2 cups lightly cooked fresh or frozen green beans, halved or cut into 1-inch lengths

½ medium orange or yellow bell pepper, finely diced

½ cup chopped carrot

2 scallions, thinly sliced

1 cup salsa, your favorite variety

¼ to ½ cup chopped black or green olives, optional

1 tablespoon olive oil

Juice of ½ to 1 lime, to taste

1 teaspoon ground cumin

¼ cup chopped fresh cilantro or parsley

Salt and fresh ground pepper, to taste

1. Combine the quinoa with 2 cups of water in a small saucepan. Bring to a slow boil, then lower the heat, cover, and simmer for 15 minutes, or until the water is completely absorbed.

2. Transfer the quinoa to a large mixing bowl to cool slightly. (If need be, speed up the cooling process by refrigerating it briefly. You want the quinoa to be slightly warm.)

3. Once the quinoa is just warm, combine it with the remaining ingredients in the mixing bowl and stir together. Transfer to a serving bowl or serve straight from the mixing bowl.

OPTIONAL ADDITIONS

- Serve over a bed of mixed baby greens, baby spinach or arugula, or tender Boston or bibb lettuce, and garnish with halved cherry or grape tomatoes.

- For a yum factor, add a medium-size firm, ripe avocado, peeled and diced.

- For an even heartier salad, add cooked or canned beans—1½ to 2 cups cooked, or a 15-ounce can of black, pinto, or pink beans (drained and rinsed).

Indonesian-Style Composed Vegetable Platter with Coconut Peanut Sauce

4 to 6 servings

This composed platter is inspired by the Indonesian dish *gado-gado*. Translated literally as "mix-mix," that's just what this dish is—a mélange of raw and cooked vegetables, arranged in separate mounds on a platter and served with a rich peanut-coconut dressing.

1 tablespoon safflower or another neutral vegetable oil

1 tablespoon soy sauce or tamari

1 (8-ounce) package tempeh (any variety)

FOR THE VEGETABLES

2 medium red-skinned or golden potatoes

4 ounces slender green beans, trimmed, or whole frozen green beans, thawed

2 heaping cups bite-sized cauliflower florets

2 to 3 medium tomatoes, cut into ¼-inch-thick half-circles

½ medium cucumber or ¼ hothouse cucumber, thinly sliced

2 cups thinly shredded green cabbage or 1 cup fresh mung bean sprouts, optional

Coconut Peanut Sauce or Dressing (page 203), or 1½ cups bottled peanut satay sauce

Sriracha or another hot sauce, optional

1. Heat the oil and soy sauce in a wide skillet. Add the tempeh and cook over medium-high heat until golden and crisp on most sides. Remove from the heat and set aside.

2. Scrub the potatoes and cut into 1-inch chunks. Place in a deep skillet with just enough water to keep the bottom of the pan moist. Steam over medium heat, covered, until just tender, about 6 to 8 minutes. Arrange in a mound on a large serving platter.

3. In the same skillet, arrange the green beans and cauliflower side by side without mixing them together. Add a bit more water to the pan to keep the bottom moist, cover, and steam over medium heat for 4 to 5 minutes, just until both are tender-crisp. Remove from the heat. Transfer each vegetable separately with a slotted spoon to the serving platter, arranging them in separate mounds.

4. Arrange the tempeh on the platter, along with mounds of tomato, cucumber, and cabbage, if using.

5. To serve, let everyone scoop the various components onto individual plates, then pass around the coconut peanut sauce. Also, pass around sriracha or hot sauce for those who'd like a spicier dish.

Chickpeas & Green Beans
with Mushroom Bacon

4 to 6 servings

When green beans are fresh and plentiful during the warmer months, this room-temperature dish goes well with fresh corn on the cob. Then, as the weather turns cooler and leafy salads just don't call to you, a warming potato dish, such as Skinny Scalloped Potatoes (page 63) or something as simple as Easy Oven Fries (page 67), make a great pairing.

Mushroom Bacon (page 195)

2 cups fresh green beans, cut into 1-inch lengths, or frozen (thawed) cut green beans

1 (15-ounce) can chickpeas, drained and rinsed

4 small tomatoes, diced, or 1 cup halved cherry tomatoes

½ cup chopped green pimento olives (see Note)

2 scallions, thinly sliced

1 to 2 tablespoons lemon juice, to taste

¼ cup chopped fresh parsley or cilantro, optional

¼ cup Basic Vinaigrette Dressing (page 197) or any bottled vinaigrette

Salt and freshly ground pepper, to taste

1. Prepare the Mushroom Bacon and set aside.

2. Steam the green beans in a small pan just until bright green and tender-crisp, using just enough water to keep the pan moist. Transfer to a colander and rinse with cool running water until they've stopped steaming. Drain well and transfer to a mixing bowl.

3. Add the remaining ingredients and toss to combine. Transfer to a serving bowl or platter and top with the Mushroom Bacon. Serve at once.

Thai-Inspired Tossed Salad

4 servings

I've enjoyed salads like this one at Thai restaurants, where it sometimes comes with a main dish as a generous first course. This is a fantastic companion to Asian-style noodle or rice dishes. Or, a larger portion of this salad can be the centerpiece of a meal, served with a simple protein dish, like Savory & Sweet Sautéed Tofu or Seitan (page 194).

Colorful and inviting, the standout flavors in this salad come from the pineapple and a luscious coconut peanut dressing. Anyone who's kind of "meh" about salads could very well be won over by this one.

1½ cups small broccoli florets, raw or lightly steamed

2 medium tomatoes, diced, or 1 cup halved cherry or grape tomatoes

½ medium cucumber, sliced

½ red or orange bell pepper, cut into narrow strips

2 cups fresh or canned pineapple chunks

1 large or 2 medium celery stalks, sliced diagonally

Crisp torn lettuce leaves or mixed greens, as desired

Leaves from several sprigs fresh cilantro

Coconut Peanut Sauce or Dressing (page 203) or bottled Thai peanut satay sauce, as needed

Chopped peanuts for topping, optional

1. Combine all the ingredients except for the coconut peanut sauce and the peanuts in a serving bowl and toss together.

2. Pass around the salad, the dressing, and the chopped peanuts, if using, letting everyone take as much as they'd like of each.

Vegetable Sushi Salad

4 to 6 servings

Typical sushi vegetables mingle with gingery rice and bits of nori (small pieces of toasted, and sometimes seasoned, seaweed; see Note) in this offbeat cold dish. The combination is positively addictive, and won't set you back as much as going out for a sushi dinner.

3½ to 4 cups cooked rice, your favorite variety, at room temperature

⅓ cup sesame-ginger dressing, bottled or homemade (page 198), plus more, as needed

1 medium avocado, peeled and diced

1 cup grated carrots, or baby carrots, quartered lengthwise

½ medium cucumber, quartered lengthwise and sliced

4 pieces nori snacks (see Note), plus more for topping, as desired

Thinly sliced scallions, optional

Sesame seeds, optional

1. Combine the rice with the sesame-ginger dressing in a medium serving bowl and stir together. Let stand for 5 minutes or so.

2. Gently stir the avocado, carrots, and cucumber into the rice. Taste, then add a bit more dressing for moisture and flavor, if necessary.

3. Cut 4 nori snacks into short, narrow strips and stir them into the rice and vegetables. Cut up 4 or more to use as topping.

4. Stir the scallions and the sesame seeds into the salad, if using (or use them as garnish, if desired). Serve at once. Pass around the extra nori for individual servings.

VARIATIONS

- Substitute other vegetables for the ones listed here. Think of some that you might come across in other vegetable sushi combos, like thinly sliced radishes or turnips, sliced shiitake mushrooms, tender-crisp asparagus, or barely cooked sweet potato.

NOTE

You'll find small packages of nori snacks at most natural foods stores and supermarkets. If you're not familiar with this product, it's exactly what it sounds like—small pieces of toasted (and sometimes seasoned) nori seaweed, the kind that's used to make sushi rolls. Two brands I like are Annie Chun's and Sea Tangle Snacks. Look for them in the snack aisle of natural foods stores.

Colorful Cabbage, Baked Tofu & Apple Slaw

6 servings

Think of this as a supercharged slaw, made more substantial with baked tofu. The sweet and tart flavors offer a fantastic contrast to creamy or spicy dishes.

3 cups shredded green cabbage or bagged coleslaw

2 cups shredded red cabbage

1 large Granny Smith or another crisp apple, cored and diced or thinly sliced

2 large stalks celery or bok choy, sliced

1 (8-ounce) package baked tofu (any variety), cut into ½-inch dice

⅓ cup raisins or dried cranberries, optional

3 tablespoons lemon or lime juice

2 tablespoons maple syrup or agave

1 tablespoon olive oil

Salt and freshly ground pepper, to taste

2 tablespoons sunflower seeds, optional

1. Combine all the ingredients in a serving bowl and toss until combined well.

2. Cover and let stand for about 15 minutes, then taste and adjust the lemon juice and syrup balance before serving.

VARIATION

- Replace the lemon juice, syrup, and olive oil with ⅓ to ½ cup vegan mayonnaise for a creamy slaw.

Simple Slaws

Coleslaw is one of the most versatile of side salads, an American classic that can be varied in so many ways. Whether you start with a head of green cabbage, one of the most budget-wise vegetables, or a bag of precut coleslaw (which can't be beat for convenience), there are a slew of ways to vary your slaws. Not only that, it's one of the few kinds of salads that actually improves as a leftover. It stays nice and crisp, and often, the flavors continue to meld. Move over, soggy lettuce and tomatoes!

For a batch of coleslaw that serves about six, you can start with 4 to 5 cups of shredded green cabbage or precut coleslaw. Then, add two or three of the following embellishments. You may want to stick with a certain theme; for example, corn kernels and bell peppers would go well in a slaw together, but corn kernels and raisins might not. The added vegetables harmonize nicely with herbal flavors, while the fruity ingredients work well with nuts and seeds. There are no rules; experiment and serve your slaws with endless variations, or find out what you and your household like best, and stick with your favorites.

Other Vegetable Additions
- Fresh or (thawed) frozen corn kernels
- Bell pepper (any color), thinly sliced
- Grated carrots
- Red cabbage (just a little, so the slaw doesn't turn lavender)
- Thinly sliced kale

Herbs
- Chopped fresh parsley, dill, cilantro, scallions, and/or chives

Fresh and Dried Fruits
- Thinly sliced apple
- Thinly sliced pear
- Raisins or dried cranberries

Nuts and Seeds (use for topping so they don't get soggy)
- Toasted sunflower or pumpkin seeds
- Toasted slivered or sliced almonds
- Chopped walnuts
- Chopped peanuts
- Trail mix with both nuts and dried fruits

Dressings
- Vegan mayonnaise
- Basic Vinaigrette Dressing (page 197)
- Sesame-Ginger Dressing (bottled or homemade, page 198)

Vegan on a Budget

Potato Salad with Red Beans & Artichokes

4 to 6 servings

Potato salads are a mainstay of summer meals, but this flavorful and filling recipe can be enjoyed any time of year. With the addition of red beans, it's satisfying enough to be a main course, though it's welcome as a side dish in smaller portions or packed into a container as a portable lunch.

Though the yum factor in this potato salad is provided by marinated artichoke hearts, you can substitute briny olives for those intermittent bursts of flavor. Or add them to the mix. For a summer dinner, this potato salad is perfect with fresh corn and a midsummer vegetable, like green beans.

4 large or 6 medium golden or red-skinned potatoes, scrubbed

½ medium zucchini, halved lengthwise and thinly sliced, or 1 small zucchini, sliced

6-ounce jar marinated, quartered artichoke hearts, drained, liquid reserved

1 (15-ounce) can red, kidney, or pink beans, drained and rinsed

¼ cup chopped fresh parsley or cilantro

2 scallions, thinly sliced

½ cup Basic Vinaigrette Dressing (page 197) or bottled, or as needed

1 cup halved cherry tomatoes

Salt and freshly ground pepper, to taste

1. Scrub the potatoes well and microwave them in their skins until done but still firm. Plunge them into a bowl of cold water.

2. Combine the zucchini in a serving bowl with the artichoke hearts, beans, parsley, and scallions.

3. When the potatoes are cool enough to handle, cut them into bite-sized chunks and add to the serving bowl.

4. Add the vinaigrette, a little of the reserved liquid from the artichoke hearts, and tomatoes. Stir together gently. Season with salt and pepper and serve.

Buffalo Cauliflower
& Chickpea Salad

4 servings

In the vegan world, either tofu or cauliflower is the go-to substitute for Buffalo hot (chicken) wings, and, of course, the dressing is dairy free. Recently, cauliflower and chickpeas have become a popular "Buffalo" combination, and this is my hot and cool salad version. The must-have ingredient, as in any kind of "Buffalo" dish, is Frank's® hot sauce—an inexpensive item shelved with other hot sauces in the supermarket. It has the remarkable ability to envelope something chewy, like the cauliflower and chickpeas here, and add a nice spicy contrast to the cool dressing and salad accompaniment. This combination platter offers a heaping portion and is fast and easy to prepare. (If you'd prefer to serve this dish as soft tacos, see Variation.)

FOR THE HOT BUFFALO CAULIFLOWER AND CHICKPEAS

- 1 (16-ounce bag) frozen cauliflower, completely thawed
- 1 tablespoon olive oil
- 1 (15-ounce) can chickpeas, drained and rinsed
- 2 to 4 tablespoons Frank's® hot sauce, or to taste

FOR THE DRESSING
(OR USE BOTTLED, SEE NOTE)

- ½ cup vegan mayonnaise
- 2 tablespoons lemon juice
- 2 tablespoons nondairy milk or water
- 1 teaspoon all-purpose seasoning
  Freshly ground pepper

FOR THE COOL SALAD

- 2 packed cups thinly sliced cabbage (green or red)
- 2 packed cups thinly sliced lettuce
- 1 cup grated carrots or baby carrots, quartered lengthwise
- 2 large or 3 medium celery stalks, thinly sliced or matchstick cut

1. Prepare the Buffalo cauliflower and chickpeas: Cut the cauliflower into very small florets. Heat the oil in a stir-fry pan or wide skillet. Add the cauliflower and chickpeas, then add enough of the hot sauce to achieve a hot and spicy kick to your liking. (If you're new to this kind of hot sauce, start with 2 tablespoons and increase as desired once the mixture starts to heat up. It's supposed to be hot and spicy, but not more than you'd enjoy.) Cook over medium-high heat, stirring often, until lightly browned in spots, about 10 minutes.

2. If you're making the dressing, combine all the dressing ingredients in a small bowl and stir together.

3. Make the salad: Combine all the salad ingredients in a bowl and toss to combine. Pour in the dressing and stir until evenly coated.

4. To serve, scoop the salad onto individual plates or into shallow bowls, and then top with some of the cauliflower mixture straight from the pan; or, you can arrange the salad on a large platter and place the cauliflower mixture on top of it, letting everyone serve themselves.

NOTE

It's not always easy to find vegan ranch dressing, but if you happen to come across it, you can use it instead of this dressing.

VARIATION

- In addition to serving the hot and cool components of this recipe as a salad, you can combine them in soft tacos, using fresh corn or flour tortillas. Scoop each of the components into the middle of the tortilla, fold it over, and, just like that, you've got Buffalo cauliflower soft tacos.

VARIATION

- For a heartier dish (and if you're not serving this with a bean dish), add 1½ to 2 cups of cooked beans, or a 15-ounce can of black, pinto, or kidney beans (drained and rinsed).

Salsa Pasta Salad
with Corn & Avocado

6 to 8 servings

Has pasta salad gone out of style? Maybe not entirely, but I don't see it served as often as I did, say, a decade or two ago. I'd like to lobby for a comeback, because pasta salads are a frugal cook's friend, and they can be enjoyed all year round. Here, your favorite salsa and a basic vinaigrette team up to offer lots of flavor. Think of this salad as a change of pace from sandwiches. And, if you'd like to make this more of a main dish, you can add some beans (see Variation).

8 ounces pasta (any short shape)

1½ to 2 cups fresh corn kernels (from 2 ears; or use frozen)

1 bell pepper (any color), cut into short, narrow strips

2 medium firm, ripe tomatoes, finely diced

2 limes

1 medium firm, ripe avocado, peeled and diced

⅓ cup Basic Vinaigrette Dressing (page 197) or bottled

1 cup salsa, your favorite variety

¼ cup chopped fresh cilantro or parsley

1 to 2 scallions, thinly sliced

Salt and freshly ground pepper, to taste

1. Cook the pasta according to the package directions until al dente. When the pasta is nearly done, plunge the corn, fresh or frozen, into the cooking pot, and cook for another minute or so. Drain and rinse under cool water, then drain well again.

2. Combine the pasta and corn with the bell peppers and tomatoes in a large serving bowl.

3. Juice one of the limes and cut the other into wedges for serving. Toss the avocado with a little of the lime juice (to keep the avocado from turning brown; discard extra juice) and add to the serving bowl.

4. Add the remaining ingredients. Toss gently and thoroughly. Garnish with the lime wedges and serve at once.

Pasta "Tofuna" Salad

8 or more servings

When I was growing up, well before I ever heard the word "vegetarian" (let alone "vegan," which only came into common usage years later), I was never crazy about eating any kind of meat or fish. One of the few things that was tolerable to me, however, was my mom's pasta and tuna salad, which she made during the summer months. Much later, when I was cooking for my own family, I updated it to use baked tofu in place of the tuna. Then, my son added a host of vegetables and herbs, transforming it into a wonderful warm-weather main dish. This family favorite recipe makes a hefty amount, so it's a good choice for potlucks and last-minute company. Leftovers make a tasty container lunch, and, believe it or not, even an offbeat and filling breakfast.

1 pound pasta (any short shape, like twists or shells)

1 (8- to 10-ounce) package baked tofu, finely diced

3 large celery stalks, diced

½ medium cucumber, diced

1 to 2 cups thinly sliced cabbage

2 scallions, thinly sliced

¼ cup chopped fresh parsley

½ cup vegan mayonnaise, or as desired

Juice of ½ to 1 lime or lemon, or to taste

1 tablespoon white or red wine vinegar

1 to 2 teaspoons Italian seasoning, to taste

Salt and freshly ground black pepper to taste

1. Cook the pasta according to the package directions until al dente, then drain. Rinse under cool running water until it stops steaming, then drain well again.

2. Combine the pasta with all the remaining ingredients except for the salt and pepper in a large serving bowl and toss together until completely mixed. Season with salt and pepper, toss again, and serve.

Kale Caesar Salad with Spiced Chickpeas

6 servings as a main dish; 8 servings as a side dish

In the vegan universe, kale Caesar salads are a staple, but, that said, they can be varied in myriad ways. In this particular rendition, for instance, spiced chickpeas, instead of the traditional croutons, are used as the topping. While there are a number of steps to this recipe, they're all easy, and the time it takes to make this hearty cold dish is fairly negligible. The result is an inexpensive, nourishing, and satisfying salad to use as a main dish or to serve as a side.

FOR THE SPICED CHICKPEAS

- 1 (15-ounce) can chickpeas, drained and rinsed
- 1 teaspoon olive or another vegetable oil
- 1 tablespoon maple syrup or agave nectar
- 1 tablespoon soy sauce
- 1 teaspoon barbecue seasoning (for more information, see page xxiii)

FOR THE DRESSING
(OR USE A BOTTLED VEGAN RANCH)

- 1 tablespoon olive oil
- ½ cup vegan mayonnaise
- 2 tablespoons lemon juice
- ½ teaspoon salt-free seasoning (for more information, see page xxiii)

FOR THE SALAD

- 6 to 8 kale leaves, laci nato or curly green, stemmed and sliced
- Olive oil for massaging the kale
- 1 medium head romaine lettuce
- 1 yellow or orange bell pepper, cut into narrow strips

1. Prepare the spiced chickpeas: Combine all the spiced chickpea ingredients except for the barbecue seasoning in a medium skillet. Cook over medium-high heat, stirring often, about 8 minutes, or until the chickpeas are nicely glazed.

2. Add the barbecue seasoning and cook for 2 to 4 minutes longer, or until lightly browned. Remove from the heat and transfer to a serving bowl.

3. Make the dressing, if using homemade: Combine all the dressing ingredients in a small bowl and stir together.

4. Make the salad: Put the kale in a serving bowl. Rub a small amount of olive oil onto your palms and massage the kale leaves for 30 to 60 seconds, until they turn bright green and soften.

5. Slice the romaine crosswise into ribbons. Add to the kale in the bowl, along with the bell peppers. Pour the dressing over the salad mixture and toss until everything is evenly coated.

6. Distribute the kale salad among individual bowls or plates and top each with some of the chickpeas. Or, arrange the salad on a serving platter, top with the chickpeas, and let all your guests serve themselves.

Hot & Cool
Black Bean Taco Salad

4 servings

If you've been perusing this chapter, you've already discovered that I have a thing for salads that combine hot and cool elements; this is one of my favorites. It's a fast, fun main dish that has it all—salad veggies, high-protein black beans, and two ingredients that add a yum factor, good-quality tortilla chips and vegan cheese.

You can make this as mild or as spicy as you'd like, depending on the kind of salsa and even the vegan cheese you choose. For a light summer meal, I like to serve this with corn on the cob and finish with fresh fruit and vegan ice cream. For a heartier cold-weather meal, a big batch of Roasted Root Vegetables with Brussels Sprouts (page 72), Easy Oven Fries (page 66), or simple baked sweet potatoes go well with this salad.

About 4 cups mixed greens or shredded lettuce, or as needed

Juice of 1 lime

2 small tomatoes, diced

1 medium-size firm ripe avocado, peeled and diced

1 (15-ounce) can black beans, drained and rinsed

1 cup salsa (your favorite variety)

Natural stone-ground tortilla chips, as needed

1 cup cheddar or vegan pepper jack cheese shreds

Chopped cilantro, optional

Sliced fresh jalapeños, optional

1. Divide the greens among 4 medium-sized plates or shallow bowls. Squeeze half of the lime juice over the greens.

2. Combine the tomatoes and avocado in a small bowl and toss gently with the remaining lime juice.

3. Combine the beans and salsa in a small saucepan or covered microwave-safe container, and heat until piping hot.

4. Distribute the prepared ingredients in layers over each of the 4 salads, in the following order: some tortilla chips, one-quarter of the black beans and salsa, one-quarter of the cheese, and one-quarter of the tomato and avocado mixture. Garnish with some cilantro and/or jalapeños, if using, and serve at once. Or, let everyone assemble their own salad.

Vegan on a Budget

Fattouche
(Middle Eastern Pita Bread Salad)

4 to 6 servings

This classic Middle Eastern salad may not be as well-known as tabbouli, but it is every bit as good. Its characteristic ingredient is pita bread, which mingles deliciously with ripe tomatoes and a simple olive oil–and–lemon dressing. It's a fantastic salad to serve with *Mujaddara* (page 39).

2 large pita breads (or see Variation)

3 or 4 flavorful ripe tomatoes, diced

1 medium cucumber, peeled, quartered lengthwise, and sliced (cut away seeds if watery)

3 to 4 scallions, minced

¼ cup chopped fresh parsley, or more to taste

2 tablespoons olive oil, preferably extra virgin

Juice of 1 lemon

½ small head dark green or romaine lettuce, shredded

Salt and freshly ground pepper, to taste

1. Preheat the oven (or a toaster oven) to 375°F.

2. Cut the pita breads into 1-inch squares with kitchen shears or a sharp knife and arrange on a baking sheet. Toast in the oven until golden and turning crisp, about 8 minutes.

3. Combine the remaining ingredients in a serving bowl and toss together. Add the toasted pita and toss again. Serve at once.

VARIATION

- Use a couple of big handfuls of lightly crushed pita chips instead of the pita bread. The salad won't be as pretty, but it works!

7

BREAKFAST & BRUNCH
SERVED ALL DAY

The recipes in this chapter feature foods that are associated with hearty breakfasts, but can be enjoyed any time of day. In fact, most of us are too rushed on weekday mornings to deal with much more than toast, hot cereals, smoothies, or grab-and-go baked goods, and that's fine, as long as these choices are made with whole foods. If this hectic morning scenario sounds familiar, you just might want to save these recipes for more leisurely weekend breakfasts or brunches. Or, if you enjoy breadfast-type dishes for dinner, there are plenty of options, like the vegetable-filled tofu scramble, that even the most weary cook can manage after a busy day. And if you make the incredibly easy and yummy breakfast cake in the evening for the next day's breakfast, feel free to enjoy a slice as an evening treat or midnight snack.

Veggie-Filled Tofu Scrambles

3 to 4 servings

For tofu fans and hard-core vegans, the breakfast and brunch repertoire wouldn't be complete without a vegetable tofu scramble. Keep these scrambles in mind for any meal of the day, though; they're as good for a simple dinner as they are to start the day. Here's a basic recipe with lots of vegetable choices (see Variations).

Vegetables of your choice (see Variations)

1 (14-ounce) tub firm or extra-firm tofu

2 teaspoons olive oil or vegan butter

½ to 1 teaspoon curry powder (for color)

Salt and freshly ground pepper, to taste

1 to 2 tablespoons nutritional yeast, if using

Sriracha or another hot sauce, optional

1. Prepare and set aside the vegetables of your choice (see Variations).

2. Cut the tofu crosswise into 6 slabs, then blot very well on clean tea towels or paper towels.

3. Heat the oil in a wide skillet or stir-fry pan. Crumble the tofu with your hands into the skillet and sprinkle on the curry powder. Sauté over medium-high heat, stirring often, until the tofu begins to turn golden, 6 to 8 minutes.

4. Stir in the vegetable(s) of choice and season with salt and pepper.

5. Stir in the nutritional yeast, if using. Serve at once, passing around the hot sauce, if desired.

VARIATIONS

Add from one to three of the following vegetables to your scramble, in whatever combinations you'd like. Some of my favorite combos are broccoli and tomato; scallions and baby spinach; and onions and bell peppers. The quantities given here are guidelines, but feel free to add more or less.

- **BROCCOLI:** Before starting the scramble, combine 1 to 1½ cups of finely chopped broccoli and a small amount of water (just enough to keep the pan moist) in the skillet you intend to use for the scramble. Cook over medium heat, stirring frequently, until bright green. Drain off any excess liquid. Transfer to a plate or bowl, then add to the scramble in step 4.

- **HARDY GREENS:** Before starting the scramble, stem and thinly slice 6 to 8 ounces of kale, collard greens, or chard. Steam the greens with a small amount of water in the skillet you intend to use for the scramble, just until bright green. Drain off any excess liquid, and transfer to a plate or bowl. Add to the scramble in step 4.

- **TENDER GREENS:** No prep is needed unless you want to rinse your triple-washed baby greens. Baby spinach, baby arugula, or watercress can be added to the skillet once the scramble is done, in step 4. Cover and allow the tender greens to just wilt, then stir in with the tofu.

- **MUSHROOMS:** Before starting the scramble, clean and slice 6 to 8 ounces of cremini (baby bella) or white mushrooms. Wilt the mushrooms down in the skillet you intend to use for the scramble, about 4 to 5 minutes, then drain off any excess liquid. Proceed with the recipe as directed.

- **TOMATOES:** Before starting the scramble, dice 2 medium-size ripe tomatoes, or cut a cupful of cherry or grape tomatoes into halves. Add to the scramble in step 4.

- **SCALLIONS:** Before starting the scramble, simply slice scallions thinly (white and green parts). Add to the scramble in step 4.

- **ONIONS:** Sauté a medium-size or large chopped onion in a little olive oil or vegan butter in the skillet you intend to use for the scramble. Then proceed with the recipe as directed.

- **BELL PEPPER:** Sauté one or two chopped medium-size red or green bell peppers (or one of each) in a little olive oil or water in the skillet you intend to use for the scramble. Then proceed with the recipe as directed.

Southwestern Tofu Scramble

4 servings

With its lively flavors, this is a vegan version of a traditional Southwestern egg dish known as *migas* (a word meaning "crumbs" in Spanish, referring to bits of corn tortilla). Tofu replaces the eggs in an altogether yummy dish that's made extra hearty with black beans.

1 (14-ounce) tub firm or extra-firm tofu

1 tablespoon olive oil

6 corn tortillas, torn or cut into approximately 1-inch pieces

1 cup salsa (your favorite variety)

1 (15-ounce) can black beans, drained and rinsed

2 to 3 scallions, thinly sliced

1 teaspoon ground cumin, or more to taste

½ to 1 teaspoon curry powder (for color)

Salt and freshly ground pepper, to taste

2 tablespoons nutritional yeast, optional

¾ cup vegan cheddar or pepper jack cheese shreds, optional

1. Cut the tofu crosswise into 6 slabs, then blot very well on clean tea towels or paper towels.

2. Heat the oil in a wide skillet or stir-fry pan. Crumble the tofu with your hands into the skillet. Cook over medium-high heat, stirring often, until the tofu begins to turn golden, 6 to 8 minutes.

3. Add the tortillas, salsa, beans, scallions, cumin, and curry, and stir together gently. Cover and cook over medium heat, stirring occasionally, for 6 to 8 minutes.

4. Season with salt and pepper and stir in the nutritional yeast, if using. If you are using the cheese, sprinkle it on top and cook, covered, until melted, 2 to 3 minutes longer. Remove from the heat and serve.

Chickpea Flour Omelets
or Frittatas

Makes 3 omelets or 3 frittatas

There's something about re-creating egg dishes in vegan versions that's fun to do and comforting to eat. As vegans, we sometimes miss certain dishes from our childhoods, and chickpea flour (often labeled garbanzo flour) helps to do the trick in the egg department. (Luckily, it's more economical than you'd expect.) While these omelets or frittatas aren't "eggs-act" replicas, they don't have to be—they're tasty in their own right. With with its pale yellow color and mild flavor, chickpea flour replicates egg batter when combined with an equal amount of liquid.

Use this basic recipe as a jumping-off point by experimenting with your own fillings, toppings, herbs, and seasonings. The frittatas or omelets are excellent for brunch, as portable lunches, or as a light dinner served with fresh whole grain bread and a salad. This recipe doubles easily.

Vegetables of your choice
(see Variations)

1 cup chickpea (garbanzo) flour

2 tablespoons nutritional yeast, optional

1 teaspoon baking powder

½ teaspoon curry powder

¼ teaspoon salt

1¼ cups water or unsweetened nondairy milk

1 tablespoon olive oil or melted vegan butter, plus more for cooking

Vegan cheese shreds (any variety), optional

Salsa, sriracha, or another hot sauce for serving, optional

1. Prepare and cook, if necessary, the vegetables you'd like to use (see Variations).

2. Combine the chickpea flour, the nutritional yeast, if using, baking powder, curry powder, and salt in a mixing bowl. Stir together until combined well.

3. Make a well in the center of the flour mixture and pour in the water or nondairy milk and 1 tablespoon of olive oil. Whisk together until the batter is completely smooth. If it is too thick, add just a little more water; it should have the consistency of pancake batter.

4. Heat enough olive oil to coat the bottom of a nonstick omelet-sized pan (8 or 10 inches wide) until hot enough to make a drop of the batter sizzle.

FOR THE OMELETS

1. Cook the omelets, one at a time: If you're using a 10-inch skillet, ladle ¾ cup of the batter into the pan; if you're using an 8-inch skillet, ladle in ½ cup. Quickly tip the pan from side to side to spread the batter, then cook over medium heat until the top firms up and the underside is golden. (Don't overcook or the omelet will crack when you fold it.)

2. Flip with a spatula and cook the other side, just until the bottom is golden. Top with your prepared vegetables and a small sprinkling of the vegan cheese shreds, if using, and fold over. Transfer the omelet to a plate and cover to keep warm. Make more omelets with the remaining batter. Serve at once, passing around the salsa, sriracha, or another hot sauce, as desired.

FOR THE FRITTATAS

1. Cook the frittatas, one at a time: Stir 1 cup of prepared vegetables (see Variations) into the batter. If you're using a 10-inch skillet, ladle about 1½ cups of the mixture into the pan; if you're using an 8-inch skillet, ladle in about 1 cup. Quickly tip the pan from side to side to spread the batter, then cook over medium heat until the top firms up and the underside is golden brown. Flip with a spatula and cook the other side, just until the bottom is golden. Transfer the frittata to a plate and cover to keep warm. Make more frittatas with the remaining batter. Serve at once, passing around the salsa, sriracha, or another hot sauce, as desired.

VARIATIONS

VEGETABLE FILLINGS: Before starting to cook either omelets or frittatas, prepare the vegetables you'd like to use in them. Each omelet can hold about ½ cup of vegetables, while each frittata can hold 1 cup. I like to combine two different vegetables, but feel free to use any number you'd like.

LIGHTLY STEAMED VEGETABLES:

- Sliced mushrooms
- Finely chopped asparagus
- Finely chopped broccoli

- Finely diced zucchini
- Finely chopped spinach or other greens

SAUTÉED VEGETABLES:

- Finely chopped onions
- Finely diced bell peppers

VEGETABLES THAT REQUIRE NO PRECOOKING:

- Thinly sliced tomatoes
- Finely chopped fresh herbs (parsley, cilantro, dill, scallions, chives, fresh oregano)

Ultimate Tofu Eggless Salad

4 to 6 servings

Tofu is the chameleon of the food world, taking on many forms and flavors. This dish has the look and feel of egg salad, though it's not intended to fool anyone—it's delicious in its own right. Serve between slices of bread as a sandwich, or just on top of bread slices, or stuffed into a pita. Shredded lettuce, green sprouts, or baby greens make it that much better. I enjoy having this eggless salad for breakfast, though it's an ideal lunch, too, served with fresh fruit.

1 (14-ounce) tub firm or extra-firm tofu, drained

1 large stalk celery, finely diced

1 scallion, thinly sliced, or several chives, chopped

⅓ cup vegan mayonnaise, or more, to taste

2 teaspoons prepared yellow mustard

1 teaspoon curry powder, or more, to taste

2 to 3 tablespoons nutritional yeast, optional

1 tablespoon pickle relish, optional

Salt and freshly ground pepper, to taste

1. Slice the tofu into 6 slabs crosswise and blot well on paper towels or clean tea towels. Place the tofu in a mixing bowl and mash well with a large fork or potato masher, or simply crumble with clean hands.

2. Add the celery and scallions.

3. Combine the mayonnaise, mustard, curry powder, and the nutritional yeast and/or relish, if using, in a small bowl and mix well.

4. Add the mayonnaise mixture to the tofu mixture and stir until combined well. Season with salt and pepper to taste. Serve at once as suggested in the headnote. Store any unused portion in an airtight container and refrigerate. This will keep for up to 3 days.

Next-Level
Vegan Hash Browns

4 to 6 servings

Potato and tofu hash browns have long been part of my weekend culinary repertoire as a late breakfast or brunch. But, truth be told, this dish is just as good for dinner, especially taken to the next level with greens and tomatoes. It's so simple and not seasoned in any special way, but the combination of ingredients makes it cozy and comforting.

If you have your potatoes cooked or microwaved ahead of time, this will be on the table in no time. Serve with whole grain toast and fresh fruit (or fruit salad), any time of day.

4 to 5 medium or 3 large potatoes

1 (14-ounce) tub extra-firm tofu

2 tablespoons olive oil, divided

4 to 5 ounces baby spinach or other baby greens

2 medium or 4 small tomatoes, diced

Paprika

Salt and freshly ground pepper, to taste

1. Bake or microwave the potatoes in their skins until done but still quite firm. When cool enough to handle (ideally at room temperature), peel and cut into large dice.

2. Cut the tofu crosswise into 6 slabs. Blot well between paper towels or clean tea towels, then cut into ½-inch dice.

3. Heat 1 tablespoon of the olive oil in a wide skillet or stir-fry pan. Add the tofu and cook over medium-high heat, stirring often, until golden on most sides, about 8 minutes.

4. Add the potatoes and drizzle in the remaining tablespoon of oil. Continue to cook over medium-high heat, stirring often, until the potatoes and tofu are golden brown to your liking.

5. Stir in the greens (in batches, if necessary), cover, and cook for a minute or two, until just wilted.

6. Stir in the tomatoes and sprinkle in a generous dusting of paprika. Season with salt and pepper and serve.

Vegan Cheese Grits
with Greens & Tempeh Bacon

4 servings

Here's an offbeat dish for a weekend brunch or an anytime dinner. Grits, a product derived from dried corn, can be somewhat off the radar, but they can add variety to your grain repertoire. Stone-ground grits, which I highly recommend, are more flavorful than stripped-down, quick-cooking grits. See the Variations for using cornmeal polenta, if you'd like to give that option a spin.

1 cup grits, preferably stone-ground

1½ tablespoons vegan butter

1 cup vegan cheddar or pepper jack cheese shreds, plus a little extra for topping

Salt, to taste

FOR THE TOPPING

5 to 6 ounces leafy greens (kale, collards, spinach, or baby power greens)

1 tablespoon olive oil

½ recipe Tempeh Bacon (page 196) or 4 to 6 strips of packaged tempeh bacon, cut into small bits

2 medium tomatoes, diced

Freshly ground pepper, to taste

1. Bring 4 cups of water to a gentle simmer. Slowly whisk in the grits, stirring constantly to avoid lumps. Cook gently over low heat for 15 to 20 minutes, or until tender and thick. (Or, follow the package instructions, as cooking times vary depending on the coarseness of the grind.)

2. While the grits are cooking, prepare the topping: If you're using kale or collards, strip the leaves away from the stems, then chop or cut into ribbons and rinse. For spinach or baby greens, just rinse.

3. Heat the oil in a skillet or stir-fry pan. Add the tempeh bacon and sauté for a few minutes over medium heat, stirring, until it just starts to turn golden. Add the greens and cover. (If you're using kale or collards, lift the lid and stir occasionally until tender but still bright green, 6 to 8 minutes. If you're using spinach or baby greens, just a minute or two will do until wilted.)

4. Stir in the tomatoes and cook for a minute or so longer, then remove from the heat. Season with pepper to taste.

5. When the grits are done, stir in the corn kernels, if using (see Variations), vegan butter, and vegan cheese. Cook for another minute or two, until the cheese is fairly well melted. Season with salt to taste.

6. Distribute the grits among four bowls and top with the greens and the tempeh bacon mixture. Sprinkle with additional cheese, if desired, and serve.

VARIATIONS

- Substitute coarse polenta cornmeal, which is quite similar to grits, for the regular or stone-ground grits. Cook according to the package directions.
- Add 1 to 1½ cups lightly cooked fresh or frozen corn kernels to the cooked grits.

Fruity Whole Grain Breakfast Bowl

1 serving (increase as needed)

There's nothing fancy or unique about this recipe, and, in fact, it's more of an idea—no need to measure anything precisely, that is. If your preferred grain takes a long time to cook, like steel-cut oats or brown rice, you may want to cook up a large batch ahead of time for a quicker breakfast. Your cooked grain will keep in the refrigerator, tightly covered, for up to 3 days This recipe serves one person, but you can easily double or triple it to serve as many as needed.

About 1 cup cooked grain (see Variations)

½ cup unsweetened or vanilla nondairy milk

1 tablespoon maple syrup or agave, or to taste

½ teaspoon cinnamon

1 teaspoon vegan butter

¼ cup raisins or dried cranberries, optional

Fresh fruit, as desired (see Optional Toppings)

Nuts or seeds, as desired (see Optional Toppings)

1. Cook the grain of your choice, according to the package directions. When the grain is nearly done (or if you're reheating it), add the nondairy milk and cook until absorbed.

2. Remove from the heat, then stir in the syrup, cinnamon, and vegan butter.

3. Transfer to a shallow serving bowl and top with the raisins or cranberries, and/or any of the fresh fruits and nuts and seeds you desire. Serve warm.

VARIATIONS & OPTIONAL TOPPINGS

■ **GRAINS:** Brown rice, quinoa, oats (quick-cooking, rolled, or steel-cut), bulgur, quick-cooking barley, or farro.

■ **FRESH FRUIT:** Bananas, apples, pears, strawberries, kiwi, mango, blueberries, or other berries.

■ **NUT AND SEEDS:** Chopped walnuts, sliced almonds, sunflower seeds, pumpkin seeds.

Savory Whole Grain Breakfast Bowl

4 servings

A quick-cooking cereal, like oatmeal or a multigrain blend, makes a hearty breakfast, but there are some people, yours truly included, who don't want anything sweet for breakfast. That's where these savory breakfast bowls come in handy. Topped with tempeh, avocado, and greens, these bountiful bowlfuls will keep you going for a good part of the day.

FOR THE COOKED CEREAL

About 4 cups cooked quick-cooking whole grain cereal (see Variations)

Vegan butter, as desired

Salt to taste

½ recipe Tempeh Bacon (page 196) or 4 to 6 strips of packaged tempeh bacon, cut into small bits

FOR THE GREENS

6 to 8 ounces kale, chard, collards, or baby spinach

Salt and freshly ground pepper, to taste

FOR THE TOPPINGS (USE ANY OR ALL)

1 medium avocado, peeled and sliced

Nutritional yeast

Sriracha or another hot seasoning

1. Make the cereal: Cook the cereal of your choice according to the package directions. When it's done, stir in a little vegan butter and season with salt to taste.

2. Make the Tempeh Bacon and set aside half the recipe for another use. Or cut into small bits packaged tempeh bacon.

3. Prepare and cook the greens: Stem and chop the kale, chard, or collards and rinse well (the baby spinach just needs to be rinsed). Combine the greens and a little water in the same skillet used for the tempeh, cover, and steam until tender, but still nice and green. Drain off any excess liquid, then season with salt and pepper.

4. Distribute the cooked cereal evenly among 4 bowls, then top each with one-quarter of the tempeh and greens. Top with any of the toppings, if desired. Serve at once.

VARIATIONS

■ For this recipe, a hearty five- or seven-grain cereal that combines a variety of grains (some might include oats, rye, barley, and others) is less mushy than oatmeal, cooks quickly, and is more flavorful and filling. However, if desired, you can just use your favorite oatmeal, steel-cut oats, or other whole grain cereal. Or, you can use quinoa or brown rice instead of cooked cereal, especially if you have leftovers in the fridge.

French Toast Casserole

6 servings

Whenever you have a houseful of weekend guests or any large group of family or friends, a breakfast casserole may be just the ticket, assuming that everyone (other than the gluten-free crowd) will be up for vegan French toast. This generous casserole saves a lot of dipping and frying and keeping slices warm—everything's done at the same time, and everyone can dig in at once. A day-old loaf of crusty French or Italian bread works best.

1 cup chickpea (garbanzo) flour

2 cups unsweetened nondairy milk (plain or vanilla)

¼ cup maple syrup, plus more for individual servings

2 tablespoons melted vegan butter

1 average-size French or Italian bread, cut into 1-inch cubes

½ cup granola (purchased in bulk, or Big Batch Granola, page 166)

Cinnamon for topping

Fresh fruit of your choice (see Optional Fruit Additions

1. Preheat the oven to 375°F and oil a 9- × 13-inch baking dish.

2. Combine the chickpea flour with the nondairy milk in a large bowl and whisk together until smooth. Stir in the syrup and melted vegan butter.

3. Place the bread cubes in a large mixing bowl. Add the chickpea flour mixture and stir quickly to coat. Let stand for a few minutes to allow the bread to absorb some of the liquid.

4. Pour the mixture into the prepared baking dish and pat down evenly. Top with the granola and a sprinkling of cinnamon.

5. Bake for 30 to 40 minutes, or until the top begins to turn golden and crusty. Remove from the oven and top, as desired, with fresh fruit. Cut into squares to serve and pass around extra maple syrup.

OPTIONAL FRUIT ADDITIONS (COMBINE ANY TWO):

- 1 peeled and sliced banana
- 1 medium peeled and sliced apple
- 1 medium sliced pear
- 1 cup hulled and sliced strawberries
- 2 medium sliced peaches or nectarines
- 1 cup whole blueberries, raspberries, or blackberries

Fruity Breakfast Cake

Makes 6 to 8 wedges or 8 bars

While this cake is super-easy to prepare, it's ideal to make the evening before you want to serve it, especially if you are looking for a grab-and-go breakfast.

FOR THE BOTTOM LAYER

1 medium banana, mashed

½ cup peanut butter

¼ cup nondairy milk

1½ cups quick-cooking oats (oatmeal)

½ teaspoon cinnamon

FOR THE FRUIT LAYER

2 heaping cups fresh fruit of your choice (see Variations)

½ cup fruit preserves (see Variations)

FOR THE TOPPING (OR USE GRANOLA IF YOU HAVE SOME ON HAND)

½ cup quick-cooking oats (oatmeal)

¼ cup raisins

¼ cup sunflower or pumpkin seeds, or finely chopped nuts

1. Preheat the oven to 375°F and lightly oil an 8-inch-square or -round cake pan.

2. Prepare the bottom layer: Mash the banana in a medium mixing bowl. Add the remaining ingredients and stir together until completely blended.

3. Transfer the oat mixture to the prepared cake pan and pat down evenly.

4. Prepare the fruit layer: Combine the fruit and preserves of your choice in the same bowl used for the oat mixture and stir until combined. Distribute evenly over the oat mixture in the pan.

5. Top the cake: Sprinkle the top evenly with the ½ cup of quick-cooking oats, followed by the raisins and seeds.

6. Bake the cake for 30 minutes, or until a knife inserted into the center tests clean. Let stand at room temperature until completely cooled. If storing overnight, cover with foil or a plate and refrigerate. To serve, cut into 6 to 8 wedges or squares.

VARIATIONS

FRUIT OPTIONS (2 HEAPING CUPS NEEDED):

- In the fall and winter months, slices of apples and/or pears are especially good. In the summer, use slices of peaches, nectarines, or apricots, or any sweet in-season berries, such as strawberries, blueberries, or others.

PRESERVES OPTIONS (½ CUP NEEDED):

- Try to use a variety of preserves made from the same or similar fruit as the fresh fruit being used. For example, use strawberry jam with strawberries, or peach or apricot jam with stone fruit. However, wth apples or pears, I would suggest apricot or peach preserves.

Big Batch Granola

Makes about 8 cups

Packaged or bulk granola is good and comes in many varieties, but for real economy and freshness, there's nothing like homemade granola. Enjoy it as a cereal, or use it to top treats, like Fruity Breakfast Cake (page 165) or vegan ice cream.

6 cups rolled oats

¼ cup sesame seeds

¼ cup sunflower seeds

½ cup raw slivered or sliced almonds, or chopped walnuts

⅓ cup maple syrup or agave

1 tablespoon safflower or another neutral vegetable oil

½ teaspoon cinnamon

1 cup dried fruit of your choice (raisins, cranberries, blueberries, or sliced apple, apricots, or pineapple, or a combination)

1. Preheat the oven to 275°F and line 2 baking sheets with parchment paper.

2. Combine the oats, sesame seeds, sunflower seeds, and nuts in a large mixing bowl.

3. Combine the maple syrup or agave with the oil and cinnamon in a small container. Drizzle into the oat mixture, stirring constantly, until mixed thoroughly and evenly coated.

4. Spread the mixture on the parchment-lined baking sheets. Bake, stirring every 10 minutes or so, for 30 minutes, or until the mixture is golden and fragrant.

5. Allow the granola to cool for a few minutes on the baking sheets, then stir in the dried fruit. When completely cool, transfer to jars or other airtight containers to store. This keeps for several weeks at room temperature; though in hot summer months you might prefer to refrigerate it so that it doesn't get rancid.

8

SWEET TREATS

Nearly everyone enjoys a sweet treat from time to time; the trick is to indulge wisely, choosing those that incorporate healthy ingredients, like whole grain flours, fresh and dried fruits, nuts, and peanut butter. Ready-made desserts, whether ordered in a restaurant or purchased in a bakery—vegan or not—can be quite expensive. Multiply those costs by several people or even a household, and that indulgence can be a major budget-breaker. The desserts in this chapter can be enjoyed guilt free; they're good for you, the planet, and your bottom line.

Big Batch Brownies

Makes 24 or 32 squares

When you need a big batch of something sweet to bring to a gathering—a potluck, a friend's birthday, or another casual occasion—these easy brownies are a natural choice. This calls for a big cake pan. If you don't own one, you can use a recyclable foil pan from the supermarket, or divide the batter between two (8-inch) square pans.

3 cups whole wheat pastry or light spelt flour

1 cup natural granulated sugar

⅔ cup unsweetened cocoa powder

1 teaspoon baking soda

½ teaspoon salt

2 cups applesauce

¼ cup safflower or another neutral vegetable oil

2 teaspoons vanilla extract, optional

½ cup unsweetened nondairy milk, or as needed

1 cup vegan chocolate chips

½ cup finely chopped walnuts, optional

1. Preheat the oven to 350°F and lightly oil a 10- by 14-inch cake pan (or recyclable foil tin from the supermarket), or two (8-inch) square pans.

2. Combine the flour, sugar, cocoa powder, baking soda, and salt in a mixing bowl and stir together.

3. Make a well in the center of the dry ingredients. Pour in the applesauce, oil, and the vanilla, if using, and stir to incorporate into the dry ingredients, adding enough of the nondairy milk to make a smooth and slightly stiff batter. Stir until combined well.

4. Stir in the chocolate chips and the walnuts, if using.

5. Pour the batter into the prepared large pan (or divide between the 2 smaller pans). Bake for 30 to 35 minutes, or until the sides of the cake begin to pull away from the pan, and a knife inserted in the middle tests clean (with the exception of the melted chocolate chips).

6. Let cool completely in the pan, then cut into 24 or 32 squares.

Easiest
Peanut Butter Cookies

Makes about 16 cookies

Who doesn't love a good peanut butter cookie? Make sure your peanut butter isn't too dense so it's easy to blend with the other ingredients.

1 cup peanut butter (smooth or crunchy), at room temperature

½ cup whole wheat pastry or light spelt flour

½ cup natural granulated sugar

¼ cup unsweetened applesauce

½ cup raisins or vegan chocolate chips, optional

¼ teaspoon salt

Pinch of cinnamon, optional

1. Preheat the oven to 350°F and line 2 baking sheets with parchment paper.

2. Combine all the ingredients in a large bowl. Work together with a pastry blender or the tines of a large fork until combined well.

3. Scoop the dough up by rounded tablespoonfuls, or a bit more if you'd like larger cookies, and arrange on the prepared baking sheets (or use 1 sheet and bake in batches).

4. Flatten the dough lightly with your palm, then press down lightly with a regular-sized fork in two directions to make a criss-cross pattern.

5. Bake for 10 minutes, or until the bottoms of the cookies are golden brown.

6. Let the cookies cool on the sheet(s) until firm, then transfer them to a plate to serve. The cookies will keep, tightly covered or in an airtight container, at room temperature for 2 to 3 days.

Soft & Chewy Granola Bars

Makes 8 bars

These vegan bars feature crunchy granola in a soft dough, making them a cross between granola bars and blondies. They're a great midafternoon snack with coffee or tea, an on-the-go breakfast, or a treat to pack in lunch boxes.

1 cup whole wheat pastry or light spelt flour

½ teaspoon baking soda

Pinch of salt

½ cup applesauce (see Note)

2 tablespoons unsweetened nondairy milk

2 tablespoons safflower or another neutral vegetable oil

¼ cup peanut butter, optional (but highly recommended)

1 cup Big Batch Granola (page 166) or packaged granola

½ cup raisins or dried cranberries

½ cup vegan chocolate chips or mini chips, optional

1. Preheat the oven to 350°F and lightly oil a 9- × 9-inch baking pan.

2. Combine the flour, baking soda, and pinch of salt in a mixing bowl and stir together.

3. Make a well in the center of the dry ingredients and pour in the applesauce, nondairy milk, oil, and the peanut butter, if using. Stir until the wet and dry ingredients are combined well, forming a stiff batter.

4. Stir in the granola, raisins, and the vegan chocolate chips, if using.

5. Pour the batter into the prepared baking pan. Bake for 20 to 25 minutes, or until a knife inserted into the center tests clean (with the exception of the melted chocolate chips). Let cool completely in the pan, then cut into 8 bars.

NOTE

Instead of buying a large jar of applesauce and having most of it go to waste if you don't use it up in a short time, buy six-packs of small containers of applesauce. Each container equals ½ cup, ideal for this and many recipes. These little containers make nice lunch box snacks, too. They will keep at room temperature for quite a long time in your pantry.

No-Bake Crispy Rice & Seed Bars

Makes 9 or 12 bars

These crispy rice cereal bars are quick to prepare and provide a good-for-you treat that tastes decadent. No baking or machines required, just a bit of patience as it firms up in the refrigerator—or, if you're in a hurry, the freezer.

¼ cup maple syrup or agave

½ cup natural peanut butter, smooth or chunky

2 cups crispy rice cereal, preferably from brown rice

½ cup Big Batch Granola (page 166) or granola purchased in bulk

⅓ cup cranberries or raisins

¼ cup vegan chocolate chips, optional

¼ cup toasted sunflower seeds, optional

1. Lightly oil an 8- × 8-inch or a 9- × 9-inch baking pan.

2. Combine the syrup and peanut butter in a mixing bowl and stir together. (Make sure to use peanut butter that's not too dense; otherwise, it will be hard to mix.)

3. Add the remaining ingredients, including the chocolate chips and sunflower seeds, if desired, and stir to combine completely.

4. Transfer to the prepared baking pan. Press firmly into the pan with the back of a spatula.

5. Transfer the pan to the refrigerator and let the mixture chill until set, about an hour or so. (Or, transfer to the freezer for 30 to 45 minutes.) Cut into 9 square or 12 rectangular bars.

Sweet Potato Chocolate Cake

Makes one 9-inch-round cake, or an 8- or 9-inch-square cake

The flavors of sweet potato and chocolate are surprisingly compatible. This moist cake offers just a subtle hint of sweet potato to your taste buds. Once you've cooked and pureed the sweet potato, the recipe comes together quickly.

2 cups whole wheat pastry or light spelt flour

½ cup natural granulated sugar

2 teaspoons ground ginger

1 teaspoon cinnamon

2 teaspoons baking powder

½ teaspoon baking soda

1 cup smoothly pureed cooked sweet potato (see Note)

2 tablespoons maple syrup or agave

2 tablespoons safflower or another neutral vegetable oil

½ to ¾ cup orange juice, preferably fresh, as needed

1 cup vegan chocolate chips or mini chips

⅓ cup raisins, optional

FOR THE FROSTING (OPTIONAL)

½ cup vegan chocolate chips

1 tablespoon nondairy milk

2 tablespoons natural peanut butter, preferably smooth

Thinly sliced apple or pear for garnish, optional

1. Preheat the oven to 350°F.

2. Combine the flour, sugar, ginger, cinnamon, baking powder, and baking soda in a mixing bowl, and stir together.

3. Combine the sweet potato puree, syrup, oil, and juice in another mixing bowl, and whisk together until smooth.

4. Make a well in the center of the dry ingredients and pour in the wet mixture. Stir together until combined well. If the batter is too stiff to mix, add a small amount of additional juice, but it should remain a thick batter. Stir in the chocolate chips and the raisins, if using.

5. Pour the batter into a 9-inch-round cake or springform pan, or an 8- or 9-inch-square baking pan. Bake for 35 to 40 minutes, or until a knife inserted into the center tests clean (with the exception of the melted chocolate chips). Let cool completely in the pan.

6. If you're making the frosting, when the cake is at room temperature, combine all the ingredients in a heatproof bowl. Set it in a saucepan above gently simmering water and heat until the chips are melted enough to whisk the mixture together. Or, simply microwave for 45 seconds, then whisk together.

7. Frost the cake at once, then let it stand until the frosting cools. Garnish with thinly sliced apple or pear, if desired, then serve.

Use your favorite method for cooking sweet potatoes—bake or microwave them whole until they're soft, and when they're cool enough to handle, peel; or peel and dice, then simmer in water until soft. Puree in a food processor, adding just enough water or nondairy milk to help it along until it purees smoothly. You'll need about one large sweet potato to make 1 cup of pureed sweet potato.

- Make this with pureed pumpkin or butternut squash instead of the pureed sweet potato.

Natural Granulated Sugar

Natural granulated sugar, like natural flours, is not bleached, and that's a good thing. First of all, who needs to consume bleached foods? More to the point, one-quarter of all white sugar is refined using the animal bone-char process, a refining method that turns sugar crystals from their original, lovely tan color to white, which is not only unnecessary, it causes pollution as well. Since this kind of sugar is often sold under generic brand labels, it's impossible to know what you're getting. Please note that sugar labeled as light or dark brown is actually bleached white sugar with a little molasses added in. Many large companies have moved away from the bone char process, though some still use it. Organic sugars are pretty well guaranteed not to use this process.

The baked goods in this section use moderate quantities of sugar (if they don't rely on other sweeteners altogether), so an average-size package will last a good long time.

Silken Tofu & Avocado Chocolate Mousse

4 servings

This delightful dessert is a mash-up of two vegan classics—silken tofu chocolate mousse and avocado chocolate pudding.

1 small or ½ medium ripe avocado, pitted and peeled

1 (12.3-ounce) package firm or extra-firm silken tofu

½ cup semisweet vegan chocolate chips

¼ cup maple syrup or agave, or to taste

1 teaspoon vanilla extract, optional

1. Combine the avocado and tofu in a food processor and process until completely smooth.

2. Transfer the mixture to a small saucepan and add the chocolate chips, syrup, and the vanilla, if using.

3. Cook over medium-low heat, whisking often, just until the chocolate chips are melted.

4. Distribute the mousse among 4 dessert glasses. Let cool completely, then serve at room temperature. Or, better yet, if you can wait, chill in the refrigerator for an hour or two, then serve.

Vegan on a Budget

No-Bake Strawberry & Blueberry Crisp

4 to 6 servings

Pretty and easy to make, this dessert combines two favorite summer fruits, and you don't even need to turn on your oven. When choosing the fruit, make sure to use the best possible in-season (late spring through summer) strawberries. Scour your local farmers' market, or maybe even pick your own. It's important to use only organic strawberries, because they're one of the most heavily pesticide-sprayed crops. With blueberries, organic is preferable, but not as critical.

Keep this fruity treat in mind when company is coming and you don't have time to make something more involved. It's even more delicious topped with nondairy ice cream or Frozen Banana Ice Cream (page 187). The secret to this dessert's yum factor is the addition of strawberry preserves, which heightens the fresh fruit flavors.

⅓ cup oatmeal

⅓ cup ground or finely chopped walnuts

2 tablespoons natural granulated sugar

Pinch of cinnamon

2 tablespoons vegan butter

1 quart strawberries, hulled and sliced

½ cup strawberry preserves, preferably all-fruit

1 cup blueberries

Nondairy ice cream or Frozen Banana Ice Cream (page 187), optional

1. Combine the oatmeal, walnuts, sugar, and cinnamon in a small bowl, and stir together.

2. Melt the vegan butter in a small skillet. Add the oatmeal mixture and stir together quickly to coat, then toast over medium heat, stirring occasionally, for 3 to 5 minutes. Remove from the heat.

3. Combine the strawberries and preserves in a mixing bowl and stir together gently until the berries are evenly coated.

4. Assemble the crisp in a 9-inch pie pan in layers: Sprinkle a bit less than half of the oatmeal mixture on the bottom of the pan, arrange the strawberries on top, followed by the blueberries, then sprinkle the remaining oatmeal mixture on top.

5. Serve at once on its own or topped with the nondairy ice cream, if desired.

Classic Apple & Pear Cobbler

6 or more servings

There's apple cobbler and there's pear cobbler. Why not double the fruity pleasure by using both fruits at once? And, after making this recipe just once, I think you'll agree that the expression "easy as pie" should be changed to "easy as cobbler." Throwing together this batter is a heck of a lot less tricky than making a decent pie crust!

FOR THE FRUIT

2 medium apples (any variety)

2 medium pears, preferably bosc

¼ cup maple syrup or agave

½ teaspoon ground cinnamon

FOR THE BATTER

1½ cups whole wheat pastry or light spelt flour

½ cup natural granulated sugar

1½ teaspoons baking powder

1 cup applesauce

1 tablespoon safflower or another neutral vegetable oil

2 to 4 tablespoons nondairy milk, or as needed

Vanilla nondairy ice cream or Frozen Banana Ice Cream (page 187), optional

1. Preheat the oven to 350°F and lightly oil a 9- × 9-inch baking pan.

2. Prepare the fruit: Peel the apples and pears, then quarter lengthwise and remove the cores and seeds. Slice thinly and place in a mixing bowl.

3. Add the syrup and sprinkle in the cinnamon; stir the fruit mixture until evenly coated. Pour the fruit mixture into the prepared baking pan.

4. Make the batter: Wipe out the mixing bowl that you used for the fruit. Combine the flour, sugar, and baking powder in the bowl and stir together.

5. Make a well in the center of the flour mixture and stir in the applesauce, oil, and enough nondairy milk to make a smooth and slightly stiff batter. Stir until combined well.

6. Pour the batter over the fruit and pat down evenly with a baking spatula.

7. Bake the cobbler for 25 to 30 minutes, or until the batter is golden and firm. Let cool until just warm, then serve on its own or topped with the nondairy ice cream, if desired.

About Whole Wheat Pastry
and
Light Spelt Flour

In a book of economical recipes, aren't these products more expensive? The answer is yes, but not by so much that they become prohibitive. If you're going to use flour and sugar (in moderation), it's good to use them in as close to their natural form as possible.

Whole wheat pastry flour, which retains the bran, germ, and endosperm of the wheat grain, makes a lovely crumb in baked goods. If you're an occasional baker, even a two-pound bag of whole wheat pastry flour will last for quite a while. Another great flour for baking is light spelt flour, which is virtually interchangeable with whole wheat pastry flour. To keep them fresh, I recommend keeping them in the refrigerator, especially during warm months when you're less likely to bake.

Mini No-Bake
Chocolate Oatmeal Cookies

Makes about 18 small cookies

With just five ingredients (plus optional sesame seeds) and no cooking time, these sweet little cookies come together in a flash. If you'd like, you can vary this recipe by rolling the dough into truffle balls. Whatever the shape, these mini cookies are special enough to serve to company, especially when served with fresh fruit—stone fruits or melons in the summer; pears or apples in the fall and winter; and strawberries in the spring.

1 cup semisweet vegan chocolate chips

⅓ cup natural peanut butter (smooth or crunchy)

¼ cup maple syrup or agave

½ teaspoon cinnamon

1 cup quick-cooking rolled oats (oatmeal)

2 tablespoons sesame seeds, optional

1. Line a platter or baking sheet with wax paper or parchment paper.

2. Combine the chocolate chips, peanut butter, syrup, and cinnamon in a medium saucepan.

3. Cook over low heat just until the chocolate chips start to melt, then stir to combine the mixture. (Don't overcook or the chocolate will seize up.) Remove from the heat.

4. Add the oats and the sesame seeds, if using, and stir in quickly.

5. Continuing to work quickly, use a tablespoon measuring spoon to scoop up the mixture. Release it onto the lined platter or baking sheet with a sharp tap, then repeat until it's all used up. If you find the mixture hardening, place the saucepan back over low heat briefly until it loosens up.

6. Transfer the cookies on the platter or baking sheets to the refrigerator and chill for about an hour, until the cookies harden. Or, if you're in a hurry, place them in the freezer for 20 minutes. Arrange on a plate to serve.

Crunchy Granola
Banana Muffins

Makes 12 muffins

These hearty banana-scented muffins make a nice breakfast treat or on-the-go snack, and they are a cozy companion with a cup of coffee or tea on a cold day. Use any kind of granola from the bulk bin that has a nice selection of dried fruits and nuts. Or, if you're a regular granola user, make sure to see Big Batch Granola (page 166), which is an excellent option to use in these muffins.

2 cups whole wheat pastry or light spelt flour

2 teaspoons baking powder

1 teaspoon baking soda

1 teaspoon cinnamon

⅓ cup natural granulated sugar

2 medium ripe (even overripe) bananas, well mashed

2 tablespoons safflower or another neutral vegetable oil

1 teaspoon vanilla extract, optional

⅓ cup unsweetened nondairy milk, or as needed

1 cup granola, divided

½ cup vegan chocolate chips, optional

¼ cup raisins or dried cranberries, optional

1. Preheat the oven to 350°F and line 12 regular-size muffin tins with foil or parchment paper cups.

2. Combine the flour, baking powder, baking soda, cinnamon, and sugar in a mixing bowl and stir together.

3. Make a well in the center of the flour mixture and add the bananas, oil, the vanilla, if using, and enough nondairy milk to make a smooth, stiff batter. Stir together until thoroughly combined.

4. Stir in ⅔ cup of the granola, followed by the chocolate chips and dried fruit, if using. (Using some dried fruit is recommended if your granola doesn't contain any.)

5. Divide the batter among the lined muffin tins. Sprinkle the remaining ⅓ cup granola evenly on top of the muffins.

6. Bake for 20 to 25 minutes, or until the tops are golden and a knife inserted into the center of a muffin tests clean. Let the muffins cool in the tins for a few minutes. When cool enough to handle, transfer the muffins to a plate or rack to cool. Serve warm or at room temperature.

Carrot or Zucchini Raisin Muffins

Makes 12 muffins

It's a good feeling when you can load muffins up with veggies and they still taste like dessert. Either carrot or zucchini can be packed into these flexible muffins, which are enticing either way. Make them in the evening and enjoy them the next day as a grab-and-go breakfast, or pack a couple into each lunch box with fresh fruit, as a break from sandwiches or container lunches.

2 cups whole wheat pastry or light spelt flour

¼ cup natural granulated sugar

2 teaspoons baking powder

½ teaspoon baking soda

1 teaspoon cinnamon

½ cup applesauce

½ cup orange juice, preferably fresh, plus more if needed

2 tablespoons safflower or another neutral vegetable oil

1½ cups firmly packed grated carrot or zucchini (see Note)

½ cup raisins or dried cranberries

½ cup finely chopped walnuts, optional

Rolled oats for topping, optional

1. Preheat the oven to 350°F and line 12 regular-size muffin tins with foil or parchment paper cups.

2. Combine the flour, sugar, baking powder, baking soda, and cinnamon in a mixing bowl and stir together.

3. Make a well in the center of the flour mixture and pour in the applesauce, ½ cup of orange juice, and oil. Stir until completely mixed. If the batter is too dry, add a bit more orange juice to loosen it, but let it remain a fairly stiff batter. Stir in the carrots, dried fruit, and the walnuts, if using.

4. Divide the batter among the lined muffin tins. Sprinkle with the oats, if using. Bake for 20 to 25 minutes, or until a knife inserted into the center tests clean.

5. Let the muffins cool in the pan for a few minutes. When cool enough to handle, transfer to a plate or rack to cool. Serve warm or at room temperature.

NOTE

If you don't have a food processor, grating zucchini on a box grater is easy. Grating carrots with a flat grater can be more tedious. If you'd like, you can use pre-grated carrots, but chop them up a little, as they tend to be a bit too long.

Lemon Blueberry Muffins

Makes 12 muffins

These muffins are best made with fresh blueberries in season, but you can make them all year round with frozen blueberries. Frozen berries make the muffins look a bit purple, but they taste fantastic either way. Whenever I make them, my family consumes them in a flash.

2½ cups whole wheat pastry or light spelt flour

2 teaspoons baking powder

1 teaspoon baking soda

⅔ cup natural granulated sugar

1 cup unsweetened applesauce

2 tablespoons safflower or another neutral vegetable oil

Juice and zest of 1 lemon (see Note)

1 teaspoon vanilla extract

2 tablespoons plain or vanilla nondairy milk, plus more if necessary

2 cups (1 pint) fresh blueberries or 1½ cups frozen wild blueberries, unthawed

1 tablespoon poppy seeds, optional

1. Preheat the oven to 350°F and line 12 regular-size muffin tins with foil or parchment paper cups.

2. Combine the flour, baking powder, baking soda, and sugar in a mixing bowl and stir together.

3. Combine the applesauce, oil, lemon juice and zest, vanilla extract, and nondairy milk in a small bowl and stir together.

4. Make a well in the center of the dry ingredients and pour in the wet mixture. Stir just until combined to make a smooth, stiff batter. If necessary, add a little more nondairy milk if the batter is too stiff, but let it remain a fairly stiff batter.

5. Gently stir in the blueberries and the poppy seeds, if using.

6. Divide the batter among the lined muffin tins. Bake for 20 to 25 minutes, or until the tops of the muffins are golden and a knife inserted into the center of one tests clean.

7. When cool enough to handle, transfer the muffins to a plate or rack to cool. Serve warm or at room temperature.

NOTE

Lemon zest gives this recipe its extra sunny flavor, and it would be a shame to eliminate it. If you don't have a lemon zester, it's an inexpensive kitchen item that looks like a large file, or you can use the small blades of a box grater.

Frozen Banana Ice Cream

4 to 6 servings

Full disclosure: I ended my previous book, *5-Ingredient Vegan*, with a similar formula for making frozen banana ice cream. But I think this chapter (and indeed, this entire collection) would be incomplete without it, for two reasons: It's an ideal way to use up bananas on the verge of being overripe, or already there; and while vegan ice cream is extremely good, it is still pretty pricey. Luckily, you won't need an ice cream machine, but you will need a food processor (a mini prep will do).

4 medium ripe bananas

2 tablespoons vanilla nondairy milk, or as needed

ADDITIONAL FLAVORINGS (OPTIONAL; CHOOSE 1):

1 cup sweet ripe strawberries, hulled and halved

1 cup blueberries

2 teaspoons cocoa powder or instant coffee granules, dissolved in about 2 tablespoons additional vanilla nondairy milk or hot water

½ cup vegan chocolate chips

⅓ cup smooth natural peanut butter

1. Peel the bananas and cut them into approximately ¼-inch-thick slices. Place them in an airtight container and freeze for several hours or overnight until frozen solid.

2. Combine the frozen bananas with the nondairy milk in a food processor and process until the bananas are broken down to bits, then stop the machine to scrape down the side of the bowl. Process again until the mixture is completely smooth and creamy, adding a bit more nondairy milk, if needed.

3. Add one of the additional flavorings, if desired, and process briefly again.

4. Scrape the banana mixture into an airtight container and refreeze for an hour or two, or until firm to the touch.

5. Scoop into individual bowls or cones to serve. Store any unused portion in the airtight container in the freezer, where it will keep for at least a week.

9

A FEW BASIC RECIPES

Here are some basic recipes that are called for occasionally throughout this book. As I've mentioned, much as I believe in taking shortcuts on certain items, especially nicely flavored bottled sauces and dressings, some readers might prefer do-it-yourself options, and I'm all about offering choices.

While you might want to weigh the advantages of making rather than buying peanut sauce, for example, due to the cost of the ingredients, there are times when homemade is a clear winner, as in the case of seitan. Otherwise, factors such as availability (I've yet to find a ready-made vegan gravy), quantity (homemade hummus stretches further), and quality (ready-made vegan sour cream has yet to come into its own) should all be considered.

Introducing Seitan

If you're new to seitan, it's a traditional Asian food used as a meat substitute. If you've been vegan for a while, you might have had it in dishes like Buddha's Delight or Mongolian "Beef" in Chinese restaurants. Seitan's meaty texture lends itself to numerous preparations, especially as a substitute for beef chunks in stews, stir-fries, fajitas, kebabs, and more.

Dense and chewy, this product of cooked wheat gluten is almost pure protein, making it one of the most protein-dense plant foods. A 4-ounce serving has about 28 grams of protein—that's substantial. Obviously, though, it's not for anyone who needs to avoid gluten.

Making your own seitan is an economical option, because ready-made seitan can be a bit pricey compared with other plant proteins, like tofu or beans. Though it might seem like a bit of a project at first, it's not difficult once you get the hang of it. Try the recipe that follows if the do-it-yourself spirit moves you. The next best thing is finding a source for locally made fresh seitan. Natural foods stores and food co-ops might have it.

A Few Basic Recipes

Homemade Seitan

Makes about 2 pounds, serving 8 or more

Store-bought seitan can be quite good, or it can be shoe-leather tough, to use a non-vegan metaphor. This recipe for homemade seitan using gluten flour provides an easy and inexpensive route to a great homemade version. Though you'll find a number of variations in books and around the web (incorporating chickpea flour, nut flours, flavorings, beans, etc.), it's good to master this basic seitan recipe first, to get the feel of how it's made. Then, by all means, feel free to experiment.

Homemade seitan doesn't require much hands-on time, just a little patience for the few steps, resting time, and cooking time. If you follow the steps outlined, homemade seitan can be more tender and flavorful than the store-bought variety. Whenever I make this, I freeze half and am always happy to have it a few weeks later.

FOR THE DOUGH

2 tablespoons soy sauce or tamari

2¼ cups gluten flour (vital wheat gluten)

1 teaspoon baking powder

2 tablespoons nutritional yeast, optional

FOR THE BROTH

1 large or 2 regular-sized vegetable bouillon cubes

2 tablespoons soy sauce, tamari, or Bragg Liquid Aminos

3 to 4 slices fresh ginger or a good squeeze of bottled ginger

1. Make the dough: Combine the soy sauce and 1 cup of water in a small mixing bowl and stir together.

2. Combine the gluten flour, baking powder, and the nutritional yeast, if using, in a medium-size mixing bowl. Gradually add the soy liquid to form a stiff dough, stirring with a spoon at first, and then working together with your hands. Drizzle in a little more water if needed to moisten all the gluten flour, but make sure the dough remains stiff.

3. Turn out onto a floured board (you can use additional gluten flour for this) and knead vigorously for 2 to 3 minutes—really work it!

4. Return the dough to the larger bowl and cover with a clean tea towel. Let it rest for 10 to 15 minutes.

5. Meanwhile, make the broth: Fill a soup pot about two-thirds full with water and bring to a simmer. Add the bouillon cubes, soy sauce, and ginger, and bring to a simmer.

6. Once the dough has rested, divide it into two equal pieces and pull into narrow loaves the shape of miniature French breads. (This dough isn't easy to work with; it tends to spring back to whatever shape it's in, but do the best you can. No matter what, it will come out fine.)

7. With a sharp, serrated knife, cut each section of dough crosswise into slices no thicker than ½ inch.

8. When the broth comes to a simmer, gently drop in each slice of dough. Within a couple of minutes, the dough is going to puff up and look like it's threatening to leave the cooking pot. It will settle back; keep pushing the pieces down into the water with a wooden spoon.

9. Once all the dough is in, I like to reach in with kitchen shears and cut pieces in half that have expanded greatly, though this is optional.

10. Simmer the dough gently and steadily for 30 minutes. Scoop out pieces of seitan (reserving the broth in the pot) and transfer to a plate or cutting board. When it's cool enough to handle, slice into strips or chunks to use in recipes. (See Notes for storing any unused seitan.)

NOTES

As soon as the seitan is cut into strips or chunks, transfer whatever portion you won't be using to a container and then pour in enough broth to cover. Use within a few days or freeze. Seitan freezes very well; thaw out on the counter or in the refrigerator before using.

Save any of the tasty broth that remains to use in soups, stews, and gravies.

Savory & Sweet Sautéed Tofu or Seitan

3 to 4 servings

When I want a basic dish to boost the protein content of a meal, I usually turn to this one. My kids grew up on the tofu variation, and it continues to be a favorite. Making this with seitan is a nice change of pace and a good choice.

1 (14-ounce) tub extra-firm tofu, or 12 to 16 ounces seitan, packaged or homemade (page 192)

1 tablespoon safflower, olive, or another neutral vegetable oil

1 tablespoon maple syrup or agave, plus more as needed

1 tablespoon soy sauce or tamari, plus more as needed

FOR TOFU

1. Cut the tofu into ½-inch-thick slices crosswise to get 6 slabs. Blot well between clean tea towels or several layers of paper toweling. Cut each slab into ½-inch dice.

FOR SEITAN

1. Make sure the seitan is well drained. You can also blot it between tea towels or several layers of paper toweling; this will ensure that it browns nicely.

2. Slowly heat the oil, syrup, and soy sauce together in a skillet or stir-fry pan, stirring together as they heat up.

3. Add the tofu or seitan and stir quickly to coat. Sauté over medium-high heat until golden brown on most sides, about 10 minutes. Add more syrup and/or soy sauce to your taste, and sauté for another minute or so.

4. Sprinkle with any or all of the Optional Additions if you'd like, then serve.

OPTIONAL ADDITIONS

- Chopped fresh herbs or thinly sliced scallions
- Sesame seeds
- Your favorite spice or seasoning blend

Mushroom Bacon

4 servings

It's amazing how a crave-worthy bacon-y smell and flavor can be replicated with just a few ingredients. Even if this mushroom bacon (or the tempeh bacon that follows) doesn't exactly remind you of the real thing, the flavor and aroma (sweet, salty, and smoky) are addictive in their own right.

Many vegan bacon recipes call for liquid smoke, but I'm not a fan of that. I find its aroma quite off-putting, and it lingers unpleasantly for hours whenever I've used it. Plus, it's not easy to find. All that said, if you like liquid smoke, go for it. Personally, I prefer barbecue seasoning blends, which are readily available in the spice section of well-stocked supermarkets. The flavors are complex and delightful, not to mention economical, because a little goes a long way.

8 ounces mushrooms (see Variations), cleaned, stemmed, and thinly sliced

2 tablespoons maple syrup

1½ tablespoons soy sauce

1 tablespoon olive oil

2 teaspoons barbecue seasoning (for more information, see page xxii)

1. Prepare the mushrooms of your choice as directed before starting.

2. Combine the maple syrup, soy sauce, and oil in a medium skillet. Stir to combine.

3. When the mixture starts to bubble, add the mushrooms and stir quickly to coat. Cook over medium heat, stirring often, until they begin to brown and get crisp here and there, about 8 minutes.

4. Sprinkle in the barbecue seasoning and stir quickly to distribute. Cook for another minute or two over low heat, then remove from the heat. Use as directed in recipes.

VARIATIONS

Cremini (baby bella) are the best and most economical option for making mushroom bacon. Ordinary white mushrooms work, too, but the brown mushrooms have a better look. You can also use portobello mushrooms, which will make larger strips. Finally, if you see shiitake mushrooms on sale, grab a few for this purpose. Their per-pound price often seems excessively high, but a handful will cost next to nothing, and you can mix a few with other mushrooms.

Tempeh Bacon

4 servings

Homemade tempeh bacon is delicious when used to make TLT sandwiches or wraps; and it's a nice addition when served alongside Tofu Scrambles (pages 152 and 154), as a topping for savory hot cereals or as a topping for soups. Of course, prepared tempeh and other plant-based bacon strips are available, and are quite good, but this do-it-yourself option will save you at least a couple of bucks per batch.

The formula for Tempeh Bacon is almost identical to that for Mushroom Bacon (page 195), but a little more of the other ingredients is used. Tempeh doesn't shrink down the way mushrooms do, nor does it give off any liquid, so it needs a little extra enhancement.

1 (8-ounce) package tempeh (any variety), cut into ¼-inch-thick strips

3 tablespoons maple syrup

2 tablespoons soy sauce

2 tablespoons olive oil

2 to 3 teaspoons barbecue seasoning (for more information, see page xxii)

1. Prepare the tempeh before proceeding.

2. Combine the maple syrup, soy sauce, and oil in a medium skillet. Stir to combine.

3. When the mixture starts to bubble, arrange the tempeh strips in the skillet in a single layer. Turn the slices over, once all of them are in the skillet.

4. Cook over medium-low heat for 4 to 5 minutes, or until the underside starts to brown, then turn the slices over again. Continue to cook until the second side starts to brown as well.

5. Sprinkle half of the barbecue seasoning over the tempeh strips. Flip them again and sprinkle with the remaining seasoning. Use as directed in recipes or serve as a side dish.

Basic
Vinaigrette Dressing

Makes about 1 cup

This all-purpose dressing is my go-to for salads and slaws. It's also a delicious marinade for roasted vegetables, especially using the balsamic vinegar option.

½ cup olive oil, preferably extra virgin

¼ to ⅓ cup white or red wine vinegar, balsamic, or apple cider vinegar

1 tablespoon yellow or grainy mustard

2 teaspoons natural granulated sugar or agave nectar

1 teaspoon Italian seasoning

1. Combine all ingredients in a bottle with a tight lid and shake vigorously until thoroughly combined. Shake well before each use. This will keep in the refrigerator for several weeks, though you'll have to bring to room temperature before using (the olive oil solidifies).

Sesame-Ginger Dressing

Makes about 1 cup

This is quite a useful dressing in my kitchen. There are good store-bought versions of this dressing, but it's easy to make with pantry ingredients. The only splurge is the dark sesame oil, but if you use this dressing regularly, making your own is still more cost-effective.

⅓ cup neutral vegetable oil (like safflower or sunflower)

2 tablespoons dark sesame oil

⅓ cup rice vinegar or white wine vinegar

1 tablespoon agave nectar or maple syrup

1 tablespoon reduced-sodium natural soy sauce or tamari

1 to 2 teaspoons grated fresh ginger, to taste

1 tablespoon sesame seeds

1. Combine all ingredients in a tightly lidded bottle. Shake well before each use. Refrigerate whatever is not used at once; bring to room temperature before using.

Tofu Sour Cream

Makes about 1 cup

Good vegan sour cream seems to be one of the final frontiers in the world of dairy substitutes. Vegan cream cheese has arrived, so it would seem logical that sour cream, its cousin, should be on the horizon. Hopefully, a good prepared brand will be available on the market in the near future. Here's a simple homemade version that should hold us in good stead in the meantime.

1 cup crumbled firm or extra-firm silken tofu

2 to 3 tablespoons unsweetened nondairy milk, or as needed

1 tablespoon lemon juice, or to taste

¼ teaspoon salt, or to taste

1. Combine all the ingredients in a food processor or the companion container to an immersion blender. Process until very smoothly pureed.

2. Store any unused portion in an airtight container in the refrigerator, where it will keep for 3 days.

Tartar Dressing or Dip

Makes about ¾ cup

This veganized classic dressing is almost silly-easy. It's my favorite condiment for vegan burgers (with or without buns), and serves as a flavorful spread for wraps. It's also a wonderful dip for raw vegetables like bell peppers, carrots, celery, and broccoli.

⅔ cup vegan mayonnaise

1 tablespoon sweet pickle relish

1 tablespoon yellow mustard

1. Combine all the ingredients in a small bowl and stir together until combined well.

Teriyaki Marinade

Makes about ¾ cup

Making your own teriyaki marinade is easy, but whether it makes sense to do so depends on whether you keep these ingredients on hand as staples. If you don't, take the shortcut route and use a good bottled brand.

¼ cup soy sauce or tamari

2 teaspoons dark sesame oil

3 tablespoons agave

¼ cup white wine vinegar or rice vinegar

2 teaspoons grated fresh or squeeze-bottle ginger, optional

2 teaspoons sesame seeds, optional

1. Combine all the ingredients in a jar. Seal tightly with a lid and shake until combined well. Always shake the marinade before using. This will keep almost indefinitely in the refrigerator if well sealed.

Homemade Hummus

Makes about 2 cups; 6 to 8 servings

Hummus has had an amazing run as one of the fastest-growing snack foods in the United States (and probably beyond) after eons as a staple of Middle Eastern cuisine. If you want to enjoy it often, consider getting into the habit of making it at home, provided that you have a food processor. It's more cost-effective and, in my opinion, tastes fresher. Most ready-made hummus comes in 10-ounce containers—barely over a cup—and for a house-hold of hummus fans, that can go much too quickly.

One of the best things about homemade hummus is that you can vary it in lots of ways. Even though it's excellent straight up, I often add an extra ingredient to the basic formula each time I make it. Aside from being used as a dip for pita and raw vegetables, hummus is an ideal base for veggie-filled wraps.

1 (15-ounce) can chickpeas, drained and rinsed

¼ cup tahini (sesame paste)

1 to 2 cloves garlic, crushed (see Note)

Juice of 1 lemon

Pinch of salt

Freshly ground pepper, to taste

1. Combine all the ingredients in a food processor with ¼ to ⅓ cup of water. Process until completely smooth.

2. Add any one of the Variations, if desired.

3. Transfer to a serving bowl. Serve as a dip or spread (see headnote). Store any leftovers in an airtight container in the refrigerator for up to 4 days.

NOTE

I'm not a fan of raw garlic, so I sauté chopped garlic first in a tiny bit of olive oil until golden. You can also use garlic granules if you have some on hand, or, between you and me, skip the garlic altogether, especially if you're using any of the variations.

VARIATIONS

- Sautéed mushrooms, roasted red peppers, olives, sun-dried tomatoes, marinated artichokes, a cooked beet, fresh herbs, and spinach, are just some of the ways you can vary your homemade hummus. Add them after step 1, once the hummus is creamy, and pulse on and off until the extra ingredient or ingredients are chopped.

A Few Basic Recipes

Super-Quick No-Cook Barbecue Sauce

Makes about 2 cups

As you've learned, I don't shy away from suggesting ready-made sauces for ease of use. And, as I've mentioned, sometimes it's less expensive to use a prepared sauce than to gather all the ingredients needed to make it from scratch. But I do like to give options! It's hard to explain, but I've always made my own barbecue sauce. Part of the reason is that I've never come across a bottled sauce that completely pleased me—I often find the smoky flavor overpowering. So I rely quite a bit on this sauce, which takes mere minutes to make and uses ingredients that are pantry staples.

1 (15-ounce) can tomato sauce

3 tablespoons maple syrup

2 tablespoons soy sauce, to taste

2 tablespoons barbecue seasoning (for more information, see page xxii)

2 teaspoons sweet paprika

1. Combine all the ingredients in a mixing bowl and stir together.

2. If time allows, cover and let stand for 30 minutes or longer to allow the flavors to blend. But if you need to use it right away, go ahead—it will still be quite good.

Coconut Peanut Sauce
or Dressing

Makes about 1½ cups

Thai peanut satay sauce is widely available in the Asian foods section of supermarkets and natural foods stores. Since some of these ingredients aren't exactly cheap, you may be better off buying it bottled, especially if you don't already have them in your pantry. But it is good to have options, and this sauce is luscious.

⅔ cup natural crunchy or smooth peanut butter, at room temperature

¾ cup light coconut milk

2 tablespoons reduced-sodium soy sauce, or to taste

2 teaspoons grated fresh or squeeze-bottle ginger

½ teaspoon sriracha or another hot sauce, plus more for serving

2 tablespoons natural granulated sugar, preferably coconut sugar

Juice of ½ to 1 lime (2 to 4 tablespoons), to taste

1. Combine all the ingredients in a small mixing bowl and whisk together until well combined. Unused portion will keep for several days in the refrigerator in a well-sealed container.

Mushroom Gravy

Makes about 1½ cups

This simple gravy is a tasty way to enhance tofu, tempeh, seitan, and cooked grains. And, of course, it's delicious on mashed potatoes.

1 large or 2 regular vegetable bouillon cubes

6 to 8 ounces cremini (baby bella) or white mushrooms, cleaned, stemmed, and sliced

2 tablespoons soy sauce or tamari

2½ tablespoons cornstarch or arrowroot

Pinch of Italian seasoning, optional

2 tablespoons nutritional yeast, optional (but highly recommended)

1. Combine 1¼ cups of water, bouillon cubes, mushrooms, and soy sauce in a small saucepan, and bring to a slow boil. Turn down the heat and simmer until the mushrooms are wilted, about 5 minutes.

2. Meanwhile, combine the cornstarch with just enough water to make it smooth and pourable.

3. Slowly whisk the dissolved cornstarch into the simmering broth, stirring constantly with a whisk, until the mixture is thickened.

4. Remove from the heat and whisk in the Italian seasoning and nutritional yeast, if desired. Use at once, or cover and keep warm until needed.

ACKNOWLEDGMENTS

For a book on economy in the kitchen, I'll keep my words of thanks economically brief:

Jennifer Williams, my editor, with whom I celebrate a long and fruitful publishing partnership

Sally Ekus and Lisa Ekus, my agents, and two remarkable women

Hannah Kaminsky, a most talented food photographer

301 Digital Media, who took over ownership of VegKitchen.com, for permission to reuse food photos from the site

The editors and designers at Sterling Publishing, who always take my work to the next level

Heartfelt thanks to all!

PHOTOGRAPHY CREDITS

All photography ©Nava Atlas except:

©BigStock: vi, 4, 22, 33, 38, 66, 73, 105, 110, 131, 152, 170, 191, 194, 197;

©Getty Images: Aamulya: xvii; Pinkybird: xv; TommL: xi;

©Hannah Kaminsky: 47, 51, 70, 105, 127, 128, 148;

©Stocksy: Ina Peters: xix; Kristine Weilert: xxv;

METRIC CONVERSIONS

Get metric equivalents for volume, temperatures, and weights for all of your most commonly used cooking and baking measurements right here.

Volume

US	METRIC
1 teaspoon	5 ml
1 tablespoon	15 ml
¼ cup	60 ml
⅓ cup	80 ml
⅔ cup	160 ml
¾ cups	180 ml
1 cup	240 ml
1 pint	475 ml
1 quart	.95 liter
1 quart plus ¼ cup	1 liter
1 gallon	3.8 liters

Temperature

To convert from Fahrenheit to Celsius: subtract 32, multiply by 5, then divide by 9

FAHRENHEIT	CELSIUS
32° F	0° C
212° F	100° C
250° F	121° C
325° F	163° C
350° F	176° C
375° F	190° C
400° F	205° C
425° F	218° C
450° F	232° C

Weight

US	METRIC
1 ounce	28.3 grams
4 ounces	113 grams
8 ounces	227 grams
12 ounces	340.2 grams

Excerpted from The Good Housekeeping Cookbook
(Hearst Books/Sterling Publishing).

INDEX

ABOUT THE AUTHOR

Nava Atlas is the author of many best-selling vegetarian and vegan cookbooks, including *5-Ingredient Vegan*, *Wild About Greens*, *Vegan Holiday Kitchen*, *Vegan Soups and Hearty Stews for All Seasons*, and many others. Nava also creates visual books on women's issues and runs two websites, The Vegan Atlas (theveganatlas.com) and Literary Ladies Guide (literaryladiesguide.com). She lives in the Hudson Valley region of New York State.